Church Administration
Effective Leadership for Ministry

Charles A. Tidwell

BROADMAN PRESS
Nashville, Tennessee

Unless otherwise stated, all Scripture quotations are from the King James Version of the Bible.

Scripture quotations marked RSV are from the Revised Standard Version of the Bible, copyrighted 1946, 1952, © 1971, 1973.

Scripture quotations marked NASB are from the *New American Standard Bible.* Copyright © The Lockman Foundation, 1960, 1962, 1963, 1968, 1971, 1972, 1973, 1975, 1977. Used by permission.

Scripture quotations marked Williams are from *The New Testament, a Translation in the Language of the People* by Charles B. Williams. Copyright 1937 and 1966. Moody Press, Moody Bible Institute of Chicago. Used by permission.

Scripture quotations marked ASV are from the American Standard Version of the Bible.

Library of Congress Cataloging in Publication Data

Tidwell, Charles A.
  Church administration.

  Bibliography: p.
  1. Church management. I. Title.
BV652.T53   1985   254   85-6620
ISBN 0-8054-3113-6 (pbk.)

To
my parents
Elmer C. and Elva Wright Tidwell
loving and beloved models
of
effective Christian administration

Contents

Preface

This book was written for anyone who wants it. But there are certain persons for whom it is primarily intended.

The major audience in mind is the person who is already in a place of church leadership or who is anticipating a leadership responsibility. Persons in either category whould be continuing students of administrative leadership. Pastors, other church ministers, church leaders in general, and many who minister in other agencies which exist to assist churches should find this text useful.

There are numerous organizations not in the "religion sector" whose leaders are committed to democratic, participatory processes. Their interest is solicited, and would be welcomed. Many basic concepts in the administration of a democratic effort apply somewhat universally to several sectors of society. The writer would be flattered if others were to find help in this book which is unapologetically for church administrative leaders. This might, in a small way, reciprocate for the vast contribution the writer has accumulated from those in other sectors of society.

The source of much of this text is the local congregation, and it is experience oriented. The writer is a "child of the church," having grown up in a Christian and church-centered family, and having been an active church member since professing faith in Christ at the age of nine. Indeed, readers will recognize that I have participated in the life and ministry of Southern Baptist churches for a number of years. In several places in this volume I use the organizational patterns of Southern Baptists as examples and models of how the tasks of church administration might be fulfilled within the various ministries of a local church. I hope you will be helped by these suggestions.

However, many ideas in this book come from sources other than church. They have been found through study, experience, and observation to have implications and applications for churches. No sector has an exclusive claim on truth. A right idea whose time has come cannot and should not be contained within the limits of one sphere of interest or discipline.

Such a book as this has limitations. Not the least of its limitations are the study, experience, and observation of the writer. No one person can capture all the useful thoughts even in one discipline. There is also a certain built-in obsolescence which descends upon any book the moment the type is set. At that point, this study, this observation, and this experience become incomplete. The student will realize this truth and be guided by it to further study.

The title of the book, *Church Administration—Effective Leadership for Ministry,* suggests its substantive character. But the hope is that the reader will see more than a static document setting forth the form of a lifeless structure. Hopefully, the reader will see some of the dynamic possibilities for human achievement, under God, which might be wrought by persons working together decently and in order.

Many of the written sources to which the writer is indebted will be apparent in the text. Some of these are new, and some are old. The best example of the ones not new but valid is, of course, the Holy Bible. No source has been included or deleted intentionally on the basis of its publication date.

Very few of the individuals whose lives and teaching have influenced the author will be apparent in the text, though at the time of the writing an almost innumerable host of influencers have arisen in memory to help articulate certain concepts and emphases. Teachers, students, fellow staff members in churches, at Mississippi College, at the Baptist Sunday School Board, and at Southwestern Baptist Theological Seminary; fellow church members, family members, and other friends would be on an inclusive list of those to whom I am indebted.

Illustrative of these are Joe Davis Heacock, R. Othal Feather, Tommy Bridges, William G. Caldwell, Alva G. Parks, Jerry

Privette, Homer E. Massey, John K. Durst, Norman E. O'Neal, Lewis E. Rhodes, Howard B. Foshee, Ralph C. Atkinson, Reginald M. McDonough, William E. Young, Idus V. Owensby, W. L. Howse, Raymond Rigdon, Clyde W. Humphrey, Norris L. Stampley, James G. Harris, and my parents, Elmer C. and Elva Wright Tidwell.

As always, my immediate family members have me in their debt beyond my ability to repay: Jean, my wife, and our children, Al and Evelyn. Credit these and others with any good which might be found herein. Attribute the errors and weaknesses to me; and, perhaps, a few choice ideas.

CHARLES A. TIDWELL
SOUTHWESTERN BAPTIST THEOLOGICAL SEMINARY
FORT WORTH, TEXAS

Introduction

Church administration is coming of age. Since 1950, more attention has been focused on church administration than perhaps all the prior years of church history. Church leaders and members alike are showing a growing sensitivity to the need for the work of the church to be done decently and in order.

Publications offering help in the administration of churches have increased. Seminars, conferences, and other training opportunities in church administration have become numerous. Courses in church administration have appeared with greater frequency in the curricula of some seminaries and a growing number of colleges and universities. Professional organizations for church administrators and teachers of church administration are developing with national proportions.

The heightened awareness of church leaders of the importance of the administrative function and the growth of this strategic field of church leadership have highlighted the need for a comprehensive, conceptual framework.

The development of a theory which includes the major elements of church administration and which shows the relationships of church leaders to that field and its functions is essential to the continued maturing of church administration. This book is an attempt to present major elements of such a theoretical framework.

Needs for Good Church Administration

There are many needs which call attention to the importance of good church administration and to the necessity of an adequate conceptual approach such as this book sets forth. Some of these needs are rather apparent.

A Church Needs Good Administration

A church is an organism. An organism is a complex structure of interdependent and subordinate elements whose relations and properties are largely determined by their function in the whole. The church, an organism, is a basic unit constituted to carry on the activities of its life by means of parts separate in function but mutually dependent. Such an organism requires administration—*good* administration—if it is to be very effective.

A church is of God and people.—There is an essential partnership between God and persons in the life and work of a church. Church administration concerns itself with presenting the human element in the partnership equation as a disciplined, orderly, purposeful instrument to be directed and used of God as He sees fit. *The premise of this book is that a well-administered organism is required by the very nature of the church and is likely to be more usable under God than a disorderly organism.* The maxim attributed to W. T. Conner captures this perspective: "The Lord can cut more timber with a sharp axe than with a dull one." Church administration attempts to sharpen the axe.

Church resources are limited.—Church administration concerns itself with the overall guidance provided by church leaders as they utilize the spiritual, human, physical, and financial resources of the church to enable the church to move toward fulfilling its purpose and objectives. On the human plane, church resources are limited. The limitation of resources makes the management of them more imperative. Church administration offers good management for a church's limited resources.

Churches are experiencing sagging influence and lagging pace.—The well-documented decline of the influence of churches on society, the continuing decline of participation in many churches, and other signs of the times indicate that churches are losing ground. Presently, most churches are decreasing in both numbers and percentages in relation to general population growth. If allowed to go unchecked, this trend portends the reduction of churches to mere remnants in the lifetime of some persons now living. Church administration offers no panacea to such conditions. Yet, good church administration, like Christianity itself, has not been tried and found wanting. It has not yet been tried on any large scale. Gross inefficiencies in the administrative affairs of the church glare to the observant church member, with resulting ineffectiveness.

Many churches have been administered poorly.—Henry Ford is credited with observing that he took it as a sign of the reality of "Deity" that the church had survived at all; no other enterprise run so poorly could stay in business. The concerned church administrator would ask, in the light of such a diagnosis, "How long shall we go on presuming on God?"

Many persons are experiencing an awakening in their relationships to God and to their neighbors. The time is right for such an awakening. The time is also right for churches to support those who are experiencing new or renewed commitments to Christ with a more effective stewardship of the always-limited resources at churches' disposal. Good church administration would maximize the stewardship of these resources.

Churches Deserve Good Administration

A church is part of the cause which is just and right. It is the instrument of God. It is under the lordship of Christ. It is relating the gospel in all its fullness to all the needs of the people.

A church proclaims the good news and witnesses.—This proclaiming and witnessing is not only within the walls of church buildings but beyond those walls wherever receptive people may be found. Leaders in this work of a church deserve the best guidance available, as do their co-workers and those who are the objects of their efforts. Much of this guidance can come from good administrative leadership.

A church educates and nurtures.—A church is learning, teaching, educating, and nurturing. Happily, the emphasis of this work is maturing from the often-limited question "What?" to include the question "So what?" A church desires to help make some significant things happen. A church is increasingly interested in learning that results in responsible living. This is really the gist—the essence—of Christian education. It is the function of a church which deserves the best leadership a church can discover and develop. Good church administration can lead in the discovery and development of effective leaders in learning and nurturing.

A church ministers to persons in need.—The number of persons in need continues to spiral. Their needs proliferate at a progressively faster rate. A church is a ministering organism. It attempts to minister unselfishly. This attempt merits the best guidance a church can muster. Good administration can provide much of this guidance.

A church worships God.—A church experiences His presence in an encounter which is life-changing and empowering. The members meet Him frequently and perhaps regularly in private and in corporate experience.

These encounters, in addition to providing benefits to the worshiping person as an end, also supply the stimulation, disposition, and spiritual power to enable the church to engage in all its other work—proclaiming and witnessing, educating and nurturing, and ministering. Such encounters deserve to be multiplied and enhanced. Good church administration can help significantly in multiplying and enhancing the occasions of worshiping encounter.

Church Leaders Need Help in Administration

Ministers and other church leaders find themselves subject to increasing demands for administrative effectiveness. They are increasingly caught up in administration. Many ministers report spending more than half their work time on administrative activities.

Some of those who report spending a majority of their work time on administration no doubt do so. However, some of these may only *think* they are spending most of their time on administration. There is a tendency to think you are spending more time than you actually are, if the activity is disliked, is frustrating, or is one in which you have limited skill or knowledge. Whether the situation is real or imaginary, the need exists for upgrading the administrative knowledge and skills, and perhaps the attitudes, of these leaders.

Some busy themselves with administrative activities of the lowest order. Usually they neglect some or all of the activities of a higher administrative order. These leaders would likely feel that they spend most of their time in administration. Again, some doubtless do. Some actually enjoy being busy with administrative work which requires more knowledge and skills in *doing things* than in *developing persons.* To them this seems to pose no problem. They seem to be unaware of what they might accomplish with the same expenditure of effort directed toward developing persons.

Some persons really don't enjoy doing things. They perhaps don't know how, or wish they didn't know. These people probably would be receptive to help in moving up in the order of the administrative work they do. There is hope for them! And once these leaders move up to developing people rather than doing things, they are seldom content to revert to their former state.

A few persons would probably rather continue and complain than change. The hustle and bustle of the arena of busywork has for them a thrill in its agony with which they are unwilling to part. This book, nor little else short of the miraculous, offers little help for them.

Church leaders feel the impact of changepace.—The world has become more complicated in many ways for the church leader. Many actually are spending unprecedented amounts of time and energy in administrative work. The church in the world is feeling the impact of changepace. The effects are often confusing to individuals and to institutions.

The alert church leader is much more aware of the many needs of persons than in previous times. He is more conscious of the need for response from the church. The responses from the church must be more and more sensitive. And the more sensitive the response to human need, the more complex the enterprise. The more complex the enterprise, the greater is the demand for democratic participation.

Working with people heightens leaders' tensions.—Democratic participation demands keen administrative insights. The increasing necessity of *working with people* raises the pressure on church leaders. The tensions are heightened by the fact that many leaders are happier doing what they can do alone rather than having to subject their efforts to the complications of involving other persons. Administration of a democracy calls for more than one person can do alone. Like it or not, the effective minister must learn to work with people. He must also maintain excellence in performing those parts of his ministry which he alone must do. This situation creates an annoying dilemma for some church leaders.

Improved leadership in nonchurch sectors affects the church.—The quality of leadership in other than church organizations has generally, though not universally, improved. There is a higher educational level among church members which reflects that of the general population. More church members are in places of responsible leadership in their occupations. There they are expected to perform according to increasingly high leadership standards and to employ ever more sophisticated techniques.

Many church members expect leadership intensity and quality of effort in the church comparable to that with which they work in their jobs outside the church. Some expect even better effort—the church *is* God's "business."

The pressures produced by improved leadership outside the church may be somewhat offset by the possibilities of transferring some of the good concepts and skills from members' occupational experiences to the area of church leadership. The church leader must be adept in administration to make the most of this potential. Hence, the minister is "on the spot" again. He can never afford to stop improving his ability to lead in deploying leadership resources of church members.

Churches are doing more things with and for more people.—Church programs are multiplying. Church organizations are growing more complex. Church members have heightened expectations of their leaders. Leadership is becoming more and more intricate, both in its artistic and in its scientific aspects. Physical resources demand increasing attention. Financial resources require astute handling. Guidance in all these areas is expected from the minister.

Complications of communicating seem to increase, even as media are improved and expanded. Motivating seems more difficult than ever before. The demands for better planning, better performance, better evaluation, and better guidance in every administrative function threaten to bury the minister who cannot seem to get on top of the job. The stresses brought on by this situation are not likely to diminish in the foreseeable future.

A thorough working knowledge of good church administration, accompanied by the attitudes and skills to make possible the use of this knowledge, may be the best, most hopeful option for the minister. Such knowledge, attitudes, and skills enable the leader to multiply personal energies through others and rise above the avalanche of responsibilities.

Church Leaders Need an Administrative Style of Leadership

Church leaders need to discover, accept, and develop an administrative style of leadership. The need is not a new one. Neither is the approach to the remedy. Both are apparent in history at least as far back as the Exodus. In Exodus 18:17-18 is the beginning of Jethro's counsel to his son-in-law, Moses:

> What you are doing is not good. You and the people with you will wear yourselves out, for the thing is too heavy for you; you are not able to perform it alone (RSV).

Jethro followed his consultation on administration with the promise of these benefits:

> So it will be easier for you, and they will bear the burden with you. If you do this, and God so commands you, then you will be able to endure, and all this people also will go to their place in peace (vv. 22-23, RSV).

The illustration from Exodus does not imply that a Mosaic structure suits all needs for all times. But the lessons should be clear that for leaders to endure and to get the work done, they must lead others to bear the burden too. This is the meaning of an administrative style of leadership.

Many have been slow to learn that an effective ministry is an equipping ministry. Some have been even slower in unlearning that other approaches to ministry are not only unproductive in terms of potential but border on being unbiblical. The effective ministry is an enabling ministry. The effective minister is an enabler of others. He is a leader in equipping. The equipping, enabling approach becomes his style of leadership. It is an administrative style. This concept reflects the foundational philosophy of this book.

There Needs to Be a Basic, Comprehensive Book on Church Administration

A single, comprehensive book which presents the basic concepts in effective church administration is needed. There are several such books on administration and on management which were written mainly for business, industry, education, government, and other nonchurch sectors of society. Some of these books provide rich lodes of excellent resource material for the student and the practitioner of church administration.

There are many other published materials—magazines articles, program helps, entire periodicals, units of resource materials, and sections here and there in books—which have been available for those specifically interested in church administration, religious education administration, or church business administration. Almost all of these materials have been well prepared and have made needed contributions to specialized problem areas in church administration. Many of these sources have proven helpful to this author.

There is need for a book in which the effort is made to set forth an overall theoretical, axiomatic, illustrated framework of church administration as a unitary disciplined, from the viewpoint of democratic leadership and congregational polity. This book certainly will not exhaust the possibilities. If it proves helpful as a primer, its purpose will have been served.

Author's Purpose

It is the purpose of the author that this book be an orderly, comprehensive, unified presentation of the functional areas which comprise the field of church administration, and an introduction to basic skills of the leaders who work in this field, so that the church may fulfill its divine mission in the world more effectively.

This purpose statement suggests that the appropriate, knowledgeable, skillful use of the concepts set forth herein could enable the church to fulfill its mission more effectively than would be possible without them. It does not mean to infer "success" through church administration to the exclusion of any other essential aspect of ministry.

Nature of the Book

The inherent character of this book is to be a presentation of the major general principles pertaining to the art and science of church administration. The field will be described with appropriate definitions, principles, propositions regarded as self-evident truths (maxims, axioms), suggested models, samples, cases, and other types of clarifying devices.

The emphasis is on function, as defined here: *a natural, characteristic action which is essential to the life of the organism.* The book is a description of the major functional areas of church administration and of the work of those who lead in these functional areas.

There is no intention to present a summary or a review of the many theories or the vast literature in the fields of administration or of church administration. Rather, the intent is to set forth a view and commend it to the consideration of the student.

This is not meant to be a book on any of the other forms of ministry per se—pastoral, educational, social, missionary, music, or any other. It is likely that there will be implications worthy of consideration by those in all forms of ministry.

The concepts may be applied to leadership situations of any size. Obviously, the more significant the size, scope, and value of a cause, the more important it is to lead it well.

Assumptions of the Author

A Theology of Church

It is perhaps generally true that more is assumed than is

acknowledged in a book such as this. However, certain assumptions which seem primary are acknowledged here.

The leadership of the church is the subject of this book. The term *church* appears many times. The proportion of use of the term to mean *an individual, local group of members* will be similar to the proportion apparent in the New Testament, estimated by some scholars to be 109 times out of the 115 appearances of the word.

Any writing about the work of the church might be expected to imply certain theological ideas about the church. Indeed, church administration has a theology of church as its basis for being. But there will be no effort to present a theology of church in any complete or systematic sense. Some theological premises which seem to be foundational for particular administrative concepts will be stated as an introduction to the administrative concepts. One might put all these together and have a semblance of systematic theology, but for the purposes of this book such a construction is not intentional.

Democratic Polity

Democratic polity is assumed to be the theory and form of church governmental system most receptive to the concepts set forth in the book. Because of the bias of the author and because of the anticipated major audience groups, there is a definite slant toward congregational polity.

Some prefer terms for congregational polity such as *Christocracy,* meaning that the members of a church govern themselves as they feel Christ is leading them. This term appears to stress the congregational concept of Christ-rule. Some others prefer the term *theodemocracy,* meaning a community governed by its members according to the revealed will of the Deity. The unique shades of meaning found in any of these similar concepts are included in the author's use of the term *congregational democracy.*

Baptist polity is congregational democracy.—Baptist polity is classified as congregational democracy. The chief characteristic of congregational democracy is the autonomy or self-government of an individual church. There is no connectional governing relationship between one church and another or between a church and any denominational body. The members of each church govern themselves. Final decisions rest with the vote of the members, each voting as he or she feels Christ wants.

The congregation of members is prominent. Each church is a unique entity or body with Christ as its Head. There is no governing authority exercised over an individual church by other churches singly or in groups. There is no ecclesiastical union of churches into a super church. The church at Jerusalem in the New Testament era sent counsel to younger churches, but each church determined for itself the course it would follow.

In a Baptist church, the members are together responsible and free to determine who shall be admitted as members, not of God's kingdom, but of that church. Baptist practice is overwhelmingly in favor of receiving persons into the membership based upon their profession of faith in Christ as their personal Lord and Savior as Baptists understand the Bible regarding this experience.

Members of each Baptist church may share in discovering and determining the purpose and objectives for that church under the leadership and lordship of Christ. Members also may share in developing and operating the means for moving the church toward the fulfillment of its purpose and objectives.

Baptist churches cooperate with other churches of like faith and order. They are free to cooperate with churches not of like faith and order, and some so choose. Baptist churches cooperate voluntarily with other Baptist churches in associations, state conventions, and the Southern Baptist Convention. The purposes of such voluntary cooperation are for fellowship and for conducting ministries together which a single church could not do as well or at all.

Other denominations such as Congregationalists, Adventists, and others practice congregational democracy. And there are other useful forms of democracy. There are also various forms of polity which include elements of congregational polity.

Churches of various polities may find helpful concepts herein. Perhaps all could learn from one another. Still, the primary applications of this writing are likely to be in churches with democratic, particularly congregational, polity.

Primacy of the Holy Spirit

The dominant primacy of the Holy Spirit is an assumption of this book. God and humanity are in a partnership in the church enterprise. God is operating in and through the church through the Holy Spirit. The Holy Spirit is not subject to human leadership or guidance. There is neither an attempt to preempt Him nor to direct, limit, or regiment His movement within the church. Christ is the Head of the church through the guidance of the Holy Spirit.

This book deals with the human elements of the God-people partnership in the church. No attempt which would lead persons contrary to the Spirit is intended. Unless the human elements of a church are motivated by, submitted to, and guided governed by the Holy Spirit, there is no right way to administer a church. This book attempts to present ways by which the human elements may become more usable under the leadership of the Holy Spirit. No church can get so well ordered that it can dispense with Him.

Some tend to equate disciplined human effort with an absence of reliance upon the Spirit. Certainly it is true that we can mistakenly elevate ourselves to the point that we believe we are due the credit for what God has done through Him. But to deny that we owe God our best possible efforts is to underestimate our debt to God. Disciplined human effort can be a measure of our commitment to, and even of our reliance on, the Spirit.

Some others tend to cover up an undisciplined human effort under the guise of a great reliance on the power of the Spirit. Such thinking is a sham and does not deceive the thoughtful person, much less God. The God is too small who can be thought to believe such illogic.

The best human effort which might be evoked requires the sanction of His blessing and guidance in order to make it worthy of offering to Him. One need not worry about making too good an offering of His own labors to God.

Universality of Administration Principles

It is assumed that there is a universality of principles between fields of administration in various sectors of society. In life as it really is, leaders in many fields of expertise learn from one another. Truth has a way of crossing our boundaries of convenience, distribution of labor, and even prejudices.

Church leaders need not be bothered about the non-church sources of some good ideas. If they are true and right, it does not matter whether they originated in or out of the church. The basic philosophic ideas of good administration anywhere find kinship with distinctively Judeo-Christian concepts. Good administration acknowledges and seeks to protect and to advance human worth and dignity. Leaders should exchange learning freely with any who honestly march under this banner.

Application of principles may vary.—The details and techniques of applying administration principles may differ in various sectors of society. This is true for several reasons. Chief among these reasons are the different purposes and objectives and different resources, both in kind and in quality. Still, the transferability of general truths between various sectors is valid. Such universality should benefit all who will accept the truths.

Dynamic Nature of Administrative Leadership

The practice of administrative leadership is dynamic, not static. The schema presented here is designed for action. It requires the ebb and flow of lives in relationship, purposing, and working to become who they may become, and doing what they may do.

One who discerns some sequence to the structure of the schema set forth as the field of church administration has received a message which was intended. But one must realize that neither life nor leadership affords anyone the luxury of living a "still shot"—life is more like a moving picture, and so is leadership. With each new scene there may be different relationships and emphases—even different leaders. Such is the nature of leadership in administration.

Upon completion of a thorough study of this book, students should be able to perform satisfactorily certain types of behavior. These are the goals the book seeks to enable students to accomplish. First, they should be able to recognize, recall, understand, and explain to a high degree of clarity and completeness the functional areas and basic leader skills of church administration. Second, they should be able to relate and apply to real situations in church administration the basic concepts they have learned, in a markedly more satisfying and effective way than before the study. When these goals are realized, the result should be that more people are reached for Christ, and in better ways—thus fulfilling the Great Commission. And He has promised to be with us always!

1
Church Administration— An Equipping Ministry

He has given some men to be apostles, some to be prophets, some to be evangelists, some to be pastors and teachers, for the immediate equipment of God's people for the work of service (Eph. 4:11-12a, Williams).

Ideas This Chapter Includes

Church administration definition

Why some disdain administration

Some biblical models of equipping ministry

Field of church administration described

The Church Is God's People

The church is people. They are not just *any* people. The church is God's people. They are children of God. They have received Christ, trusting in Him (John 1:11-12). They have repented to God of their sin and have professed faith in the Lord Jesus Christ (2 Cor. 7:10; Acts 20:21; 1 John 4:15). God is their Father. They are His heirs jointly with Christ (Rom. 8:17). They are no longer lost, unrepentant creatures of God. They are saved, pardoned from sin, and born again as children of God (1 John 1:9; John 3:17).

The Church Is a Voluntary Fellowship of Believers in Christ

The people who are the church have voluntarily banded together to form a fellowship of believers in Christ (1 John 1:7). Early Christians valued this fellowship highly (Acts 2:42). Paul wrote to the church at Philippi: "I thank my God upon every remembrance of you. For your fellowship in the gospel from the first day until now" (Phil. 1:3,5).

The Church Belongs to God

The church is not a mere man-made institution (Matt. 16:17-18; 1 Tim. 3:15). It belongs to God. It is a spiritual fellowship of children of God. It is characterized by members' love for one another (Gal. 4:6; 1 John 3:14). The members love God. They assemble themselves together to worship God. They encourage one another to do good works (Heb. 10:24-25).

Christ Is the Head of the Church

Christ is the Head of the body of people who are the church. "And he is the head of the body, the church" (Col. 1:18; see also Eph. 1:22; 4:15). The church body is somewhat like a human body. It has many parts. Each part has a particular contribution to make to the whole body (Eph. 4:16). Christ, the Head of this body, gives it unity, direction, balance, and control.

Some Lead in Equipping the Church for Ministry

One way Christ guides the church is through those persons who lead. Some of those who lead are ministers. Their function in leading is to equip God's children for the work of service (Eph. 4:11-12*a*). The minister or ministers of a church work in a variety of ways in order to equip the members to serve. They preach, teach, and perform other leadership services. They watch over the members like shepherds (Acts 20:28). They are God's servants as they function.

The Work of the Church Is Ministering

The church has work to do. The work is identified as serving, ministering. The ministry of the church is performed by persons. These persons give aid, help, and benefit to other persons. The nature of the aid, help, and benefit—the ministry performed—grows out of members' understanding of the purpose and objectives of the church in relation to the needs of persons.

Ministering Utilizes Resources

The work of the church utilizes resources. These resources are spiritual, human, physical, or financial. Usually there is some limit to the amount of resources available. In some instances, there are limits on quality also. The limited resources are evident in relation to the seemingly numberless needs of persons.

Definition of Church Administration

Leadership and guidance in deploying the church's limited resources for ministry are essential if there is to be optimum effectiveness. Leading the church to discover and determine its purpose and objectives is imperative. Identifying the needs of persons and designing and developing the church's responses to these needs are vital. Relating resources appropriately is crucial. The leadership and guidance required to achieve optimum effectiveness in these facets of ministry are precisely what comprise the field and function of church administration.

Church administration is the leadership which equips the church to be the church and to do the work of the church. It is the guidance provided by church leaders as they lead the church to use its spiritual, human, physical, and financial resources to move the church toward reaching its objectives and fulfilling its avowed purpose. It is enabling the children of God who comprise the church to become and to do what they can become and do, by God's grace.

Church administration may be described as a *field* in terms of certain functional areas in which leaders perform certain leader functions. To the extent that one performs these leader functions in the field of church administration, to that extent one may be termed a church administrator. A leader gives leadership.

Leadership Is Guiding Along a Way.

Leadership is the act or process of guiding someone or something along a way. It may imply going in advance of those who are being guided or led to show the way, and perhaps to keep followers under control and in order.

Guiding implies intimate knowledge of the way and of all its difficulties and dangers. Occasionally the guiding may be a single act, an accomplishment complete in itself and essentially unique. More often it is action which involves a process, a series of actions or operations conducive to an end. The actions or operations may be continuous.

Church Leadership Is Under Christ

In a church the leadership is performed by persons who are to follow the leadership of Christ, the Head of the church. He enables leaders and others to discern the way by means of the Holy Spirit's guidance.

Church Leadership Exists to Equip

The reason for leadership and guidance in a church is *to equip the church.* To equip the church is to furnish it for service or action. To equip means *to prepare, to dress, to array, to outfit.* The ancients used the word to mean setting a dislocated joint, putting it in order.

> In the verb form, it appears in Matthew 4:21—mending a tattered net. Our verse (Eph. 4:12) combines the metaphors of body and building (just as we do in the idea of body-building exercises) to suggest a tightly knit unity of function, where the work of the laity and that of the clergy are so closely interlocked that everyone together plays a decisive role.[1]

To equip is to furnish, to provide any or all essentials making for efficiency in action or use for performing a function. To equip the church is the natural, characteristic, essential action of church leadership. Such action is vital to the life of the organism, the church.

Ministry of Administration Is to Equip

Church administration exists to equip the church for ministry. The root meaning of the term *church administration* supports this view. The word *administer* comes from the Latin word *administrare* which is a combination of the prefix *ad* with the infinitive *ministrare,* "to serve." Church administration is to serve the church. The form of the service is ministry. The Latin word *minister,* from which come our words *minister* and *ministry,* literally means "servant."

The field in which the servant renders the service is the church. Hence, it is church administration. The noun *administration* is the act or process of administering. Usage has brought the concept of administration to be very similar to that of management, the judicious use of means to accomplish an end. Church administration is concerned with providing leadership in discovering and determining the ends, and guidance in the judicious use of means to accomplish the ends.

Ministry of Administration Is Equipping Persons

There is, indeed, a ministry of administration. It is a ministry of equipping persons for service. The persons equipped are the church. As leaders and co-workers discover and do the work of the church, there are "things" which must be done. Some of these things are administrative. But administration is much more than the doing of things. It is the "growing" of people. It is enabling them to lead the right people to be at the right place, with the right things, at the right time, with the right attitudes, knowledge, and skills, to perform service that is right to perform. The reader may expect the theme of "growing people" to recur throughout this book.

Why Some Disdain Administration

In the minds of many there is an undesirable connotation attached to the thought of church administration. This is noticeably true with some ministers. There is a variety of reasons to explain why they feel as they do. It will be helpful to acknowledge some of these ways of thinking. Generally, it could be said that most of the disdainful thinking about church administration stems from inadequate or inaccurate concepts of what constitutes church administration. The remainder might be attributed largely to unfortunate attitudes about oneself and/or others. Some observers might reverse the proportions of the two previous statements.

Faulty Concepts of Church Administration

To some church leaders, church administration is a conglomeration of "frazzling details" which keeps them from getting on with the ministering to which they were called. Typically, these irritating details are identified as the paperwork, office work, troublesome equipment, maintenance bothers, money problems, and other similar items which sometimes harass all ministers and almost always harass some.

Equating Administration with Poor Administration

It is admittedly difficult to envision oneself as being at the pinnacle of ministry while laboring with rolled-up sleeves over a usually cantankerous copy machine, with smeared ink gradually menacing the bottom of the roll in the sleeve. This situation, however, does not illustrate good administration but poor administration, especially if this predicament is frequent or routine. As Seward Hiltner stated in a thoughtful chapter on "The Ministry as Administration," "For some administration is poor not because it is administration but because it is poor."[2]

Almost all occupations have some tasks which may be unsuited to the taste or liking of the doer. The field of church leadership is no exception to this. Church administration has its share of toilsome work. These tasks can become almost infinitely burdensome if the minister's concept of what comprises church administration is limited to baneful work.

Preferring "Spiritual" Things

Some have the work of the church organized into spiritual and temporal. These see themselves called to work in the spiritual realm, not the temporal. They follow in the train of bygone leaders who thought that the preacher should preach and not bother (or be a bother) with things like church finances. Such mundane affairs were thought to be the just share of the laity. Such a view may have served effectively to keep the minister from becoming bogged down in details. It also served effectively in keeping him on a social pedestal in the church and community which dulled his influence on life as it is lived in the home and the marketplace. Some ministers prefer such isolation, and some churches prefer to perpetuate it.

Those who avoid giving leadership in the temporal aspects of the church apparently have missed the point that it is possible to minister (a spiritual act) to the needs of persons as together they plan and do the work of the church. This world of work may afford the minister his best channel by which to validate for his people the great truths of life he enunciates by word and manner of living. It is possible that minister and members alike might experience more Christian growth and maturing as they work together in church ministries, and the supporting services thereof, than they would by typical or traditional Christian growth programs—as important as these are. The ministry of administration rejects the artificial dualism of spiritual and temporal in the life and work of the church. Such dualism reflects an inadequate and inaccurate concept of church administration.

Rejecting "Executive Image"

Some disdain administration because they reject the "executive image" with which some others have implemented administrative responsibilities. These usually sincere persons don't want to be thought of as executives. They, too, are confusing a legitimate activity with a mistaken concept. There is no "big wheel" self-concept in the best executive. To execute is to put into effect, to carry out, to perform. An executive is one who puts into effect, carries out, performs. None of these actions is wrong. All of them are right to do. The problem is that of a great idea maligned by poor performance. It is all right to be the right kind of executive. Almost any worthy and noble function could be distorted by one who performs it in a wrong or crude manner. Such performance by some is hardly justification for avoidance of good performance by others.

Unfortunate Attitudes Toward Self and/or Others

Some disdain church administration as espoused in its best forms because of unfortunate self-concepts, or poor concepts of others, or both. To identify all of these problems would not only be beyond the scope of this treatise but would also likely tax the most competent analyst. Perhaps to point out some of these problems would serve as a mirror to some persons, thereby enabling them to see themselves, and, possibly to determine to leave the ranks here indicated. With that hope, let us proceed.

Inflated Ego Problems

Some who have a distaste for church administration have equated it with the lowly chores of the church, which they feel themselves to be above doing. These are not included in their call to minister, and they are not about to be caught doing them, even if they go undone. If the church wants these chores done, "they" can get someone else to do them, or do them themselves. These people feel called to be the "chiefs" at every gathering, and the "Indians" at none. Besides, to act like an ordinary member might lower the esteem in which the other members hold them. They might become just another person, without a lordly pedestal elevating them above the common herd.

Some are unwilling to acknowledge that they are not sufficient for every need. These are very likely as busy as one can be with administration as they see it (doing things), and despising almost every minute of it. But to call for help would be to admit that they, too, have some limitations.

Some formally educated persons who got the idea in their theoretical concept of ministry that higher education elevated them to the position of telling others what to do and expecting them to do it wonder why much of what they tell someone to do goes undone. Soon *administration* becomes a bad word for them. These have made the lofty trip up to great ideas in learning but have not engineered their lofty learning to make contact with real life. Their education has just made one direction of a two-way trip. These persons have a lot yet to learn. It is conceivable that they might learn much of what they yet lack through more formal study, if it could be the right kind. Others may learn through informal ways. This group has potential.

Low Opinions of Others

Some suffer from overwork in administrative matters be-causes of an inability or an unwillingness to rely on others to do any significant parts of the work. Some of these persons have a series of poor experiences to show for the few times they did entrust something significant to someone else. Now they feel that if they want something done right, they'll have to do it themselves. So why not just go directly and do the work themselves? These persons may turn out mountains of certain types of work but never as much as if they concentrated on multiplying their energies through others they could develop.

It is possible that someone else might do the work at least satisfactorily and, at the same time, realize a sense of vital satisfaction in service. One might even become capable of doing more difficult jobs through successes in doing less diffi-cult ones. A few might even do some jobs better than the leader. Then where would the person with ego needs look for satisfaction? How could he or she change their low opinion of others?

A low opinion of others may be reflected in other ways. One rather common way is for the leader to pretend he is involving others in significant ways in the guidance of the church but always to make sure those he involves are kept busy on small details, while he handles the strategic ones.

Still another variation of this theme is for the leader to let others go through the motions of meaningful participation in the administration of the church, particularly in matters call-ing for planning and deciding, but to be certain that the out-comes are predetermined. The duration of a given work session in this psuedo-leadership situation is just how long it takes the group to arrive at the only way acceptable to the leader in the first place. Leaders who practice this deception often confuse their successes in manipulation with high-quality church administration. They have their reward.

Hiding in "Busywork"

Some don't know how, or think they don't know how, to do those parts of their work calling for higher skills. They may hide in the busywork of church administration and consciously or unconsciously excuse themselves for poor performance in other responsibilities. These seldom make good administrators.

Wanting to Do Everything

The simple pleasure of doing everything one thinks is part of one's work can become an "ego trip." A newspaper account of the work style of a real-life minister illustrated this weakness. In performing a wedding this minister was reported actually to have done these things: donned his coveralls to clear the pews; disappeared for a quick change before coming to the organ bench to play the prelude; hurried back to march out with the groom; performed the ceremony; sang the closing prayer; raced to the vestibule, asking the people to remain in their places until he arrived there; and with one hand greeting the attenders and another pointing guests to the visitors' registry, he placed one free foot in the church bell rope and tolled the bell! When asked by an interviewer why he didn't get someone to help him, he replied that he'd rather do it all himself. The comic senselessness of this kind of behavior seems too obvious for further comment.

Views of Persons and the Church

Some cannot or will not bring themselves to approach the work of the church in a way that reflects genuine love for and confidence in people as creatures made in the image of God, with intelligence and potential for commitment and for responsible service as children of God. These have some serious cause for reexamining their view of persons and of the church. Certainly no one is perfect on the human scene. But consider Hiltner's statement at this juncture:

> There is no reflective Christian who has not at some time asked the question, "Was God out of his mind to entrust this most precious treasure to people like us and churches like ours?" And if he has answered the question rightly, he has finally said, "Yes, we are as bad as that; but God was willing to risk it, and he must know what he is doing."

If even God felt it wise and right and essential to risk his purposes and his love through fallible human instruments, who is a minister to be unwilling to acknowledge that his ministry must be risked through fallible human beings who are, in actual fact, no more fallible than he?[3]

Church Administration and People

Church Administration Involves People and Things

Church administration is bound up with people and with things. This is true even of poor administration. But a major difference in good administration and poor administration lies in the emphasis the administrator places on people as being more important than things. The position of the church leader in this choice seems simple. But the problem has some tricky subtleties in it.

Some church leaders fear that they do not relate well to people. Some actually relate poorly. This old problem remains from generation to generation. Its toll is increased because of the growing requirement that the minister relate to people in constructive and productive ways.

Studies by seminary curriculum committees and others continue to show that the biggest problem area for church leaders, specifically ministers, is their inability to relate satisfactorily and effectively to people. This is a serious flaw. It is not unique to church leaders. It is evident in most sectors of society, if not all. The problem does not disappear with a wish; neither do people.

The typical minister much prefers to spend his time and energies doing those parts of his work which he does alone, without consultation with other persons. While these aspects of his work may be said to be principally and eventually for people, the people are not present in the flesh, to be led by the minister, or to be persuaded or educated to concur, to work, to give, to serve. The work of the church increasingly requires working with people.

In preparing a sermon or a training conference session, the minister can move directly from his thought to the performance. Such direct and easy transition from thought to action is not characteristic of good administration, because good administration is leading people to grow and to develop in their knowledge, skills, and attitudes as *together* the leader and co-workers try to advance the church toward its purpose and objectives. This kind of leadership takes time and tireless effort. The net product may turn out to be quite different from what the initiating leader had in mind. A measure of personal grace is required in a leader to enable him to acknowledge that his gems of thought and planning might be altered, even improved, by group processes.

Good Administrators Specialize in Working with People

Good administration requires the leadership and guidance of persons who are specialists in working with people. These specialists get their own jobs done to the extent that they enable other persons to succeed in getting their respective jobs done. Such a leader is concerned with getting the work of the church done. But he has a primary concern with helping the people who are the church to grow and to develop in the joys and satisfactions of productive service as they reach out to minister to others. The leader must have a wholesome balance of interest in persons and in what they might produce in Kingdom service. The added benefit of the approach which puts people first is that there usually results more productivity—more of the work of the church is accomplished.

There is a treacherous pitfall to be avoided in the emphasis on people first, productivity second. It is the trap of a feigned interest in persons in order to increase their productivity. People are the business of the church and its ministers, whether or not they ever produce for the church. One could at times easily fake an interest in persons and lead them by artful manipulation toward goals which they do not share. This is unscrupulous leadership and falls outside the concept of good church administration and outside the intentions and practices of the best administrators.

Leaders Should Lead Members

The most effective church leadership has long been that which takes the equipping ministry approach. Even if a church could engage the services of enough persons whom they compensate, fully or partially, in order to free them to devote more time to doing the work of the church, and could charge them with the responsibility of doing all the church's work, and even if they were able to do it, it would not be right or wise to do. Leaders should lead all who will follow to share in the work of the church. This is the way to enable the members of the body to grow and develop and, at the same time, to advance the cause of Christ through the church. The adage is true that "It is better to put ten men to work *than to do the work* of ten."

Biblical Models of the Equipping Ministry

There are several biblical models from which there is much to learn regarding the equipping ministry concept. None of these models provides every detail needed for effective church administration. Each of them contains concepts with which good church administration is highly compatible.

The Jethro-Moses Model

An early biblical model, already mentioned in the introduction, is one given to Moses through consultation with his father-in-law, Jethro. It is recorded in Exodus 18:13-27. Careful study of the passage reveals many helpful administrative insights.

> And it came to pass on the morrow, that Moses sat to judge the people: and the people stood about Moses from the morning unto the evening. And when Moses' father-in-law saw all that he did to the people, he said, What is this thing that thou doest to the people? why sittest thou thyself alone, and all the people stand about thee from morning unto even? And Moses said unto his father-in-law, Because the people come unto me to inquire of God: when they have a matter, they come unto me; and I judge between a man and his neighbor, and I make them know the statutes of God, and his laws. And Moses' father-in-law said unto him, The thing that thou doest is not good. Thou wilt surely wear away, both thou, and this people that is with thee: for the thing is too heavy for thee; thou art not able to perform it thyself alone. Hearken now unto my voice, I will give thee counsel, and God be with thee: be thou for the people to Godward, and bring thou the causes unto God: and thou shalt teach

them the statutes and the laws, and shalt show them the way wherein they must walk, and the work that they must do. Moreover thou shalt provide out of all the people able men, such as fear God, men of truth, hating unjust gain; and place such over them, to be rulers of thousands, rulers of hundreds, rulers of fifties, and rulers of tens: and let them judge the people at all seasons: and it shall be, that every great matter they shall bring unto thee, but every small matter they shall judge themselves: so shall it be easier for thyself, and they shall bear the burden with thee. If thou shalt do this thing, and God command thee so, then thou shalt be able to endure, and all this people also shall go to their place in peace. So Moses hearkened to the voice of his father-in-law, and did all that he had said. And Moses chose able men out of all Israel, and made them heads over the people, rulers of thousands, rulers of hundreds, rulers of fifties, and rulers of tens. And they judged the people at all seasons: the hard causes they brought unto Moses, but every small matter they judged themselves. And Moses let his father-in-law depart; and he went away into his own land (ASV).

Moses was not able to get all the needs of the people met. People were waiting from morning until evening to see him. Some doubtless went away at the end of the day not having reached Moses. They might have gone away angry.

Jethro showed good judgment in his approach to Moses. He asked questions first, and later offered answers. He asked Moses *what* he was doing ("to the people") and *why* he was trying to do it alone.

Moses gave a simple, obvious answer about *what* he was doing. He seemed confused about *why* he was trying to do it alone. "The people come unto me" (v. 15). Inept administrators still try to explain their predicament like this. Some wouldn't want it any other way. And Moses, man that he was, reached for the most religious sounding reason he could honestly give for his problem: they come to me "to inquire of God" (v. 15). This was true; but subsequent developments confirm that much if not most of what was going on was simple arbitration of differences between a man and his neighbor (v. 16). Other men, with the qualities given in verse 21, could do most of this arbitrating. They later did.

Jethro bluntly told Moses that what he was doing was not

good. He also told him why it was not good: Moses and the people would surely wear away. The implication is that the people's needs would continue to go unmet. The job was too heavy for him. He could not do it alone.

Jethro Prescribed an Equipping Ministry for Moses

Jethro admonished Moses to listen to his counsel. He invoked God's presence with Moses (v. 19) and the authoritative command of God (v. 23) that Moses follow the counsel. Here are the major points of the prescription.

1. *Pray for them.*—Moses was to represent the people before God. He was to bring their causes to God. This seems to be a way of saying he was to pray for them and their problems.

2. *Teach them the guidelines.*—Moses was to teach the people the statutes and the laws. These were to be their guidelines, as policies, procedures, and rules.

3. *Show them the way.*—Moses was to show the people the way wherein they must walk. Since they had the pillar of cloud and fire for their physical direction, this admonition must refer to Moses showing them their life direction, as spiritual counselor.

4. *Show them the work.*—Moses was to show the people the work they must do. Their work was to become a nation to be used for God's redemptive purposes. The work was their challenge from God. It was to provide much of the motivation for their struggle to become the kind of instrument as a people through whom God could work. Their work was for them the "program."

5. *Organize the people into manageable groups.*—Moses was to organize the people into manageable groups. The pattern was to have groups of thousands, which, in turn, would have groups of hundreds. The hundreds groups were sub-grouped into fifties, and the fifties into groups of ten. This was their organization design.

6. *Choose qualified men to lead each group.*—Moses was to see that qualified men were provided "out of all the people" to be placed over each unit of the organization suggested. The "job qualifications" are impressive. These leaders were to be able, God-fearing, truthful, haters of unjust gain. Their span of

leadership was reasonable—each man could be expected to cover his assignment effectively.

7. *Give the chosen leaders continuing authority.*—Moses was to let the chosen leaders of the groups judge the people at all seasons. Their authority was not limited to any season. No one would benefit by waiting for a different season for his arbitration to be handled. This arrangement would expedite the solving of disputes and avoid a loaded docket. It would be an exception to the statutes and laws which would not be decided by these judges. This pinpointed responsibility both for the people and for their leaders.

8. *Have leaders decide routine matters.*—Moses was to have the chosen judges decide "every small matter." These were the routine kinds of problems which were covered by statutes and laws or which were of limited magnitude. This kind of problem was to be solved on the lowest possible level of the organization structure—at the point nearest the problem itself —where the facts of the issue were most readily apparent.

9. *Bring "great matters" to the chief leader.*—The people and/or their judges were to bring to Moses "every great matter." These would be matters of large importance which were not satisfactorily dealt with under the statutes and laws. These were the exceptions. Moses was to judge these. He was to manage by exception, a management concept which has been articulated in this century by some as though they invented it.

One who wonders how a man like Jethro could be the source of such keen insights should consider at least two factors. First, there seems to be sufficient evidence that God was initiating this counsel. Second, each suggestion Jethro made is filled with the kind of practical wisdom which might come from any objective, intelligent, thoughtful person who was not so caught up in busyness that he couldn't take time to think through the problem. Jethro's advice to Moses was not mysterious, not in a language foreign to Moses, and not without many evidences of "common sense." It was instrumental in helping Moses to move from being a mere hardworking leader with a following to being an effective administrator in his time.

The promise Jethro made to Moses as the results of installing this model of ministry are worthy of consideration in any era.

He declared that it would be easier for Moses, the chief leader. Moses needed that relief. Jethro said that others ("they") should bear the burden with Moses. This news should have been well received. He said that Moses should endure. A good administrator should last longer. He concluded that the people should go to their places in peace—implying that their needs would have been met! This is what it's all about.

The language of the last verse in the passage allows for the interpretation that Moses might have detained Jethro until the plan could be successfully initiated: "And Moses let his father-in-law depart." But the departure came after Moses had done all that Jethro had said. Moses, great though he already was, was not so "great" that he could not learn rapidly from his father-in-law. Perhaps one measure of greatness is the willingness of one to learn what one should, regardless of the source, as long as it is honest and right.

It would be easy to point out some untimely aspects of the Jethro-Moses model in applying it to democratic leadership in a church. The times have afforded some changes in situational factors which would make some of the model unsuited to the church. But a model does not have to be a perfect model in order to be instructive. For Moses' needs in his times, the counsel of Jethro was relief from a seemingly impossible situation. Much of the widsom could be suited to our time and used with great profit.

Jesus' Model of Equipping the Apostles

Jesus in His earthly ministry presented an instructive model of the equipping ministry. While no single passage of Scripture offers a comprehensive concept comparable to the Jethro-Moses model, a study of the total approach of Jesus in relation to His apostles shows Him clearly in the role of preparing them to minister. He furnished them the essentials for performing ministry. He equipped them to do "greater things than I am doing" (John 14:12, Williams). Hull stated clearly the approach of Jesus and its results:

> When Jesus launched his ministry, he bypassed the religious professionals of his day, choosing instead to recruit twelve ordi-

nary laymen from differing walks of life. To these men, who lacked the training of the rabbis or the prestige of the priesthood, he said, "You are the salt of the earth, the light of the world" (see Matt. 5:13-16). It is astonishing how they became the pivot on which hung the very survival of his movement. It is not an exaggeration to say that when Jesus died he left only two things on earth—the blood spilt in loving sacrifice for others and the impact of his life upon a handful of frightened, faltering men. The fact that they were open to the reality of his resurrection, that they were willing to overcome provincialism in carrying out a worldwide mission is testimony to the wisdom of the basic strategy Jesus followed.[4]

Hull continued, crediting Jesus' equipping strategy with the rapid movement of the church as it spread from being a tiny remnant with Judaism to become a worldwide faith. "If the twelve had viewed themselves as the only legitimate ministers, they would soon have been overwhelmed as the group they led grew from 120 to three thousand at Pentecost."[5] In fact, one might add that they very nearly were overwhelmed as the church grew, saved only by their administrative move to lead the church to choose others to share the work load with them (Acts 6). Jesus' idea had caught on.

Hazards in Identifying as Jesus

There is great value in learning from the way Jesus related to persons and in trying to emulate His compassionate, considerate manner. There are also some limitations for one who might identify *as* Jesus in one's leadership role. No one is in the same relationship with others that Jesus was with His apostles. There is a subtle hazard that one may come to see only oneself as Jesus and the other persons as "mere" apostles. This danger can express itself in a somewhat condescending manner, surely not characteristic of Jesus. And, sadly, the "apostles" often may respond as required by the leader who identifies as Jesus. One must bear in mind that each of God's children has equal claim to the privilege of identity with Jesus.

Paul Espoused the Equipping Ministry Approach

Paul clearly favored the equipping ministry approach for church leaders. From the time of his earliest team relationship as associate to Barnabas (Acts 11:19-26) at Antioch, Paul practiced and taught an equipping ministry. Strong and superbly qualified as he was for singular leadership, Paul saw the essential wisdom of a shared ministry.

God's Gifts Are to Equip God's People for the Work of Service

Paul most clearly presented the equipping ministry model in Ephesians 4:11-16. There he set forth the relationship between those persons given to be apostles, prophets, evangelists, pastors and teachers, to the people of God, the church. He identified the relationship in functional terms, not in terms of static position nor of governing authority. He plainly declared the function of the recipients of the gifts to be God's gifts to the church for "the immediate equipment of God's people for the work of service" (v. 12, Williams). Hull concluded:

> Ephesians 4:12 provides the biblical foundation for a theological concept of "equipping" which is crucial to the vitality of the church. It defines the primary work of various specialized ministries as that of completely "outfitting" all Christians so that they will be able to fulfill the service which makes the church grow in unity and strength. This concept removes any barriers between clergy and laity because it assumes that every Christian belongs to the universal priesthood (see 1 Pet. 2:5-9).[6]

Paul stated the purpose of the equipping relationship: "for the ultimate building up of the body of Christ" (v. 12b, Williams). He indicated the extent to which the purpose was to be sought: "until we all attain to unity in faith and to perfect knowledge of the Son of God, namely, to a mature manhood and to a perfect measure of Christ's moral stature" (v. 13, Williams). He continued and characterized both in positive and negative comparisons the mark of the fulfilment of the purpose of God in affording His gifts to the church (vv. 14-15). The apostle concluded the passage with the classic statement of the headship of Christ over the Church and the members properly functioning under His direction:

> For it is under His direction that the whole body is perfectly adjusted and united by every joint that furnishes its supplies; and by the proper functioning of each particular part there is brought about the growing of the body for its building up in love (v. 16, Williams).

The harmonious functioning of the church is to be achieved under the direction of Christ, through the equipping ministries of those to whom He has given the gifts, with the accompanying responsibility for exercising the gifts. He has given the gifts to persons. He gave the persons to the church. The church has the responsibility for carrying out God's assignment: "The perfecting of the Body is the work, not of 'the ministry' but of 'all the saints,' and the ministers are to prepare the saints for this work."[7]

In other passages Paul referred to this concept (see 1 Cor. 12:14-31). But a better characterization of good church administration than that which he gave in Ephesians 4 is not forthcoming. The early church expanded rapidly "because of the leverage achieved when the few with special gifts saw their task as the training of the many to exercise those gifts which belong to every believer."[8]

Church Administration Is an Equipping Ministry

Church administration truly is an equipping ministry. As church leaders understand, accept, and practice this concept of ministry, the church will be mobilized, its resources liberated, and the work of the church will be accomplished in almost unprecedented effectiveness.

Church administration, an equipping ministry, is a functional field. A field is an area of activity. The field of church administration may be viewed in several ways as one attempts to delineate it. The primary view of the field as presented in subsequent chapters of this book is to identify and describe the various functional areas which together comprise the total field.

*Identifying Some Groups in Church Administration
Helps Give Visibility*

One way of envisioning the field is to identify some of the groups which are commonly found in the activity area that is church administration. These groups represent some of the organizational forms in which administrative functions take place. Examples of these groups are these: church staff, church officers, basic church programs, and the church membership at large.

Church staff members work through others.—Staff may be defined as those persons who make their work contributions through other people not under their supervision in ways which make the other people accountable to them. Staff members in a church are usually compensated partially or fully (in terms of subsistence) for their services. Many times these persons are not only staff in functioning (working through others), but are also *line* workers in that they assume or are assigned certain responsibilities for personal production or services which they render substantially alone.

Illustrative of church staff positions are pastor, minister of education, minister of music, church business administrator, minister of youth, associate pastor, and many others.

Church officers render specialized administrative services. —Church officers are individuals chosen by a church to render specialized administrative services to the church membership at large. "Church officers usually fill positions that require only one person."9

Baptist churches commonly have these church officers: (1) a presiding officer, usually called the moderator. The pastor may or may not serve in this office. (2) A clerical officer, who is usually referred to as the church clerk. With the development of church staffs with one or more secretaries, many churches have a secretary who either works with or in place of the church clerk. (3) A financial officer, who is usually called the treasurer. Again, the treasurer may be assisted by a church staff member, such as a financial secretary. (4) Legal officers, who are called trustees. A church which is legally incorporated must designate persons to be officers of the incorporated body, some of whom most likely serve the church in one of the areas enumerated above, in addition to being officers of the corporation.

Church officers serve generally to enable the church to transact its affairs properly with its own membership, with other churches, with other church bodies, and with certain other individuals and institutions in society, notably business and governmental. Their work, and that of the persons whose work relates most closely to theirs, is largely administrative.

Basic church programs have administrative requirements. —A basic church program is a set or group of basic continuing tasks of primary importance in moving a church toward fulfilling its purpose and objectives. The leaders of these programs in many churches work together with one another and with other leaders in the church in order to advance the cause of Christ through their programs. Examples of programs identified in Baptist churches are: (1) pastoral ministries, (2) Bible teaching, (3) missions, (4) music ministry, and (5) church training.

The organizational medium for the cooperative work of the program leaders in many churches is the Church Council. Usually led by the pastor, and often assisted by other church staff members, the Church Council performs administrative services with and for the church.

Major concerns of a Church Council include helping a church discover and understand its nature and purpose, making the church program relevant to the church and community needs, helping avoid unproductive duplication and overlapping responsibilities and activities, scheduling church activities, helping plan and use resources wisely, and enriching the fellowship.

Program leaders and others whose work relates to the programs of the church are at the heart of the church administration activity. The organizations they lead are of major importance in a church. Together their work is the church's ministry, almost in its entirety.

Service programs assist the church and its programs.—Many churches have organizations to assist the church and its basic programs in strategic ways. They may be referred to as service programs. These organizations provide media services, recreation services, and administrative services.

Service programs make the work of the church and its basic programs more efficient and effective. Relating these services most appropriately to the church's total ministry is an administrative responsibility.

Church committees provide administrative services to the church.—Almost all churches do some of their work through church committees. The work performed by church committees is almost always administrative.

A committee is a group of persons designated by a parent group and assigned to perform one or more continuing or temporary specialized services which the parent group either cannot do, will not do, or chooses not to do for itself.

Generally there are two types of committees in a church. "Regular" committees work on assignments which have continuity, usually throughout the year. "Special" committees carry out assignments usually short-term and of a unique nature. Upon completion of their assignment the special committee is usually thanked and dismissed.

Churches use committees for many essential services, such as assisting in nominating workers for church offices and organizations, leading in stewardship and financial affairs, advising in matters regarding properties and space, helping with church staff administration, and many others. Work with church committees comprises a significant and large segment of the field of church administration.

Church members are the church.—The church members are the total body of persons who have been received officially into the membership of the church, with all the rights, privileges, responsibilities, and relationships pertaining thereto. Sometimes the term *congregation* is used as a synonym for "the church." *Congregation* is a less precise term for the church than what one usually means when he refers to the body, the members. A congregation is a gathering of people. The church is more than any gathering, unless the gathering includes the members.

In churches operating on the congregational polity pattern, the rights and privileges of membership usually include entering into deliberation and discussion of the church's decisions, expressing choice by voting one vote, and holding office or position for which one might be duly elected. In Baptist churches the privileges extend to participating in the ordinances of baptism and the Lord's Supper. The rights and privileges are determined by each church.

Each church also determines the responsibilities and relationships of its members with regard to the church and other entities. Churches may vary widely in their hopes, expectations, and requirements in this area. Some churches adopt a statement, either a "standard" covenant or one of their own devising, which is intended to guide particularly with regard to member responsibilities and relationships. Often the rights and privileges receive more attention of members than do the responsibilities and relationships.

The church is an administrative group.—The church is an administrative group whether gathered in a meeting or not. The church is obviously an administrative group when a valid quorum of its members is meeting to consider matters of interest to the church.

Some churches organize members into subgroups in order to make working with them a more manageable possibility. One way of determining the grouping is by the geographic location of members' residences. One or more members might be asked to serve as the contact link for members in each of the geographic subdivisions.

In Baptist churches the deacons often organize the church members into family subgroups in order to implement church ministries to and through them. There are other ways of organizing the church into subgroups which might be useful to a church.

Field of Church Administration Described

However a church might be organized, the concern of church administration is with the mutual relationships of the members with one another, with the corporate church, and with the world in which the church is placed to minister. It is likely that the total church member group is the most neglected administrative unit among the entire scheme of church groups. New emphasis is being placed upon this total unit. The emphasis is needed and deserved. Much of it is coming through the church's program of pastoral ministries. The *church is the field for church administration.*

Broadly, All Administrative Work in a Church

Broadly speaking, it is valid to include as church administration all the administrative work in a church. Not all of what occurs in the groups is administrative. Certainly there should be more than administration going on in and through the church's groups, or the administration is indeed poor. Good administration exists to help ensure that ministry will be performed according to some orderly design to reach certain needed and desired goals. Church administration is more than moving about among the groups of a church's administrative structure. It is more than dealing with the organizations, though the organizations are involved.

Church Administration as Functional Areas

To study the field of church administration in terms of functional areas seems more appropriate than to study it in terms of organizations. There are certain functional areas in which the administrative leader must function, regardless of the forms or organizations chosen to implement the action.

A functional area of church administration is a part of the field in which leaders perform certain administrative actions which are natural, characteristic, and essential to the life of the organism, the church.

A function is a natural, characteristic action which is essential to the life of the organism. In church administration a function is an administrative action and is performed in a functional area.

Functional Areas Together Comprise
the Field of Church Administration

These are the functional areas which comprise the field of church administration:

Purpose
Objectives

Program (or Ministry Plan)
Organization
Human Resources
Physical Resources
Financial Resources
Control

Church Leaders Lead in Functional Areas

In these working territories church leaders perform certain administrative actions or functions. The common thread which weaves through all the administrative functions is that the nature of the functions is *leading*. Not all administration and leading are synonymous, but all administration is related to leading, if it is good administration.

An administrator employs certain skills, techniques, and knowledge working in the privacy of his or her own thoughts and singular efforts. But one does not become an administrator until one has related in a leadership way to the church or to a part of the church. One administers in relation to persons, not things. The work of the administrator is principally leading and guiding persons.

The Administrator Performs Certain Basic Skills in Particular Functional Areas

The administrator leads and guides persons by performing certain basic skills in the particular functional areas indicated. He leads in planning, initiating, organizing, delegating, directing, motivating, supervising, performing, influencing, controlling, evaluating, communicating, and representing. An administrator sometimes might exercise all of the basic skills in a single functional area of administration. These skills are the subject matter for the last chapter in this book.

Logic and Sequence in the Functional Areas Presented in This Book

Completeness, logic, and sequence are apparent in the order of the functional areas when applied to a given instance of use. In beginning an enterprise, given one or more leaders plus persons with whom leaders are to work, a leader leads the co-workers to consider the functional areas in the order presented here. First, they consider their purpose and objectives. Once these are discovered and determined, they develop a program (or ministry plan) the implementation of which is to move them toward fulfilling their purpose and objectives. The program or ministry plan has implications for designing the organizational pattern or patterns needed. When the organizational design is completed, leaders then know the scope of the task of maximizing human resources to staff the structure.

People (human resources) often require physical resources. These must be provided. Human resources and physical resources generally call to mind financial resources. These are to be provided and husbanded. And in all of these functional areas there must be control. Control must be maintained to assure that the financial resources will be used appropriately to provide the physical resources for the human resources who staff the organization designed to implement the program or ministry plan.

The leader leads down the list of functional areas while planning. He leads up the list in implementing the plans. The action would flow as in the chart.

Plan		Implement
	Purpose	
	Objectives	
	Program (Ministry Plan)	
	Organization	
	Human Resources	
	Physical Resources	
	Financial Resources	
	Controls	

There is Dynamic Movement Among the Functional Areas

Completeness, logic, and sequence should be apparent in this "framework" of administration. But in operation there is dynamic movement among the functional areas. Church leaders do not complete their work in each functional area and then move on to the next functional area, never to return to an area previously considered.

Feasibility concerns might surface as leaders survey available human, physical, or financial resources. Insurmountable obstacles in the resources areas could cause leaders to ascend the list to alter the organization pattern, the program plan, or even the objectives and purpose. Leaders might "yo-yo" up, down, and around the order of the functional areas, now functioning in one, then in another. Occasionally they might be concerned with several functional areas related to various interests at the same time. Even so, the direction of the sequence, both in planning and implementing, serves as a base to which leaders may go to resume their movement.

The List of Functional Areas Provides as Orderly Checklist

Administrators use the orderly list of functional areas as a checklist to determine whether they are giving attention to all the major functional areas involved in a given enterprise or endeavor. The framework can be useful when applied to almost any situation, from planning and implementing a Sunday School picnic to administering the most serious and sophisticated enterprise. Some have contemplated its use in analyzing and ordering the direction of their individual lives and families.

Variety of the List of Functional Areas

1. *Ideas, people, and things.*—There are some dissimilarities on the list of functional areas. Some functional areas have to do with ideas, or even ideals, more than with persons per se. The area of purpose and objectives is an example of the preponderantly idealogical functional area. Human resources is an area that is clearly personal. Physical resources is just as clearly the area of things. The administrator is aware that the eventual concern in all the areas is persons. It is vital to distinguish between persons and things, lest one make the error of treating persons as things. The leader is always an enabler, an equipper of persons. They are the focus of ministry.

2. *Ends and means.*—There are ends and there are means on the list of functional areas. Ends are those items of ultimate value toward which the church strives and works. Means are the tools and techniques by which the church moves toward ends. Purposes and objectives are areas which qualify as ends.

Program or ministry plan, organization, physical resources, financial resources, and control are means to be used in reaching ends. Persons (who are part of the area of human resources) are not means in any insensitive way, though it is by means of persons that the church does its work under Christ. The training of persons is a part of human resources as an area, and training is a means.

Some leaders have erred in their leadership through a confusion of ends and means. They have made ends of that which should be means and vice versa. Neither program nor ministry plan, nor organization, nor physical resources, nor financial resources, nor control is worthy to become an end in itself. Administrators who either operate or appear to operate without discernment between ends and means produce undesirable and unchristian consequences, the hurt of which lingers almost infinitely. They suffer from end-means inversion. They risk what Albert Einstein phrased in characterizing this age, "a perfection of means and a confusion of goals." Such confusion is a threatening hazard which portends ill to the administrator who is its victim or its perpetrator, and to the cause of Christ and His church. This inversion has no place in church administration.

Summary

Church administration is an equipping ministry. The church is God's people. It is a voluntary fellowship of believers in Christ. It belongs to God. Christ is the Head of the body, the church.

Some are given to lead in equipping the church for ministry, which is the work of the church. Ministering utilizes resources. Effective ministering requires leadership. Church administration is leadership which equips the church.

Leadership is guiding along a way. Church leadership is under Christ. Its reason for existence is to equip. The ministry of administration is equipping persons for service.

Some persons disdain administration. Some of these have faulty concepts of what church administration is. Some equate administration with poor administration. Some prefer "spiritual" things. Some reject "executive image," a result of poor executive conduct. Some have unfortunate attitudes toward self. Some have ego problems. Some have low opinions of others. Some hide in busy work. Some love doing everything themselves. Some need to reexamine their view of persons and of the church.

Church administration involves people and things. The administrator must favor people. Many relate poorly to people. Good administrators specialize in working with people. One should avoid the trap of a feigned interest in persons.

The administrator leads members to do the work of the church. There are biblical models of this equipping Ministry Concepts. Three Models which are instructive are the Jethro-Moses model, Jesus, and Paul. The church has the assignment; leaders' assignment is to equip the church. The early church practiced this concept, and expanded thereby. Church administration is an equipping ministry.

Church administration is a functional field. That is the primary perspective of this book. However, identifying some of the groups found in church administration helps give visibility to the field. Some of these groups are the church staff, church officers, basic church programs, service programs, and the church members as a group.

The field of church administration when viewed as groups might be arranged in several clusters which classify the various groups. Broadly, all administrative work in a church is church administration.

To study church administration as functional areas seems best. A functional area is a part of the field. The administrator performs certain basic skills in the functional areas. Functional areas together comprise the church administration field. The basic leader skills together comprise leadership for ministry.

There is completeness, logic, and sequence in the order of the functional areas presented in this chapter. In a given enterprise, one leads down the list to plan, and up the list to implement plans. But there is, in reality, much dynamic movement among functional areas.

The list of functional areas also provides an orderly checklist for the administrator. Not all functional areas are of the same kind. There are ideas, people, and things represented on the list. Some are ends, and some are means. The administrator must avoid end-means inversion. Such confusion has no place in church administration, a ministry of equipping and enabling persons for ministry.

Learning Activity Suggestions

1. Interview three ministers who are serving churches presently.
   a. Write down this information from each interview:
      (1) Estimate of the proportion or percentage of work time each spends on administration.
      (2) The activities each lists as illustrative of one's administrative work.
      (3) A summary of the feelings of each regarding one's present involvement in church administration.
   b. Compare the findings of each interview with the concepts of church administration presented in this chapter.

2. Read chapter 4, "The Ministry as Administration," in the book *Ferment in the Ministry,* by Hiltner. Write a paragraph or two of your reaction to the content.

3. Write a treatise in 1,000 words or slightly less, in which you reflect your thinking and study concerning church administration as an equipping ministry.

4. Study Ephesians 4:11-16, using five or more versions and commentaries as desired. Then write your own paraphrase.

5. What is your response to the "functional areas" approach to the field of church administration? What changes would you make in listing your own version of the functional areas?

Notes

1. William E. Hull, "Equipping: A Concept of Leadership," *Church Administration,* January, 1972, p. 7.

2. Seward Hiltner, *Ferment in the Ministry* (Nashville: Abingdon Press, 1969), p. 72.

3. Ibid., p. 85.

4. Hull, p. 6.

5. Ibid.

6. Ibid.

7. W. O. Carver, *The Glory of God in the Christian Calling* (Nashville: Broadman Press, 1949), p. 150.

8. Hull, "Equipping," p. 6.

9. Howard B. Foshee, et al, *The Work of Church Officers and Committees* (Nashville: Convention Press, 1968), p. 9.

2
Purpose of Church

The Lord of hosts has sworn:
"As I have planned,
so shall it be,
and as I have purposed,
so shall it stand,
that I will break the Assyrian in my land,
and upon my mountains trample him under foot;
and his yoke shall depart from them,
and his burden from their shoulder.
This is the purpose that is purposed concerning the whole
    earth;
and this is the hand that is stretched out
over all the nations.
For the Lord of hosts has purposed,
and who will annul it?
His hand is stretched out,
and who will turn it back?" (Isa. 14:24-27, RSV).

Of this gospel I was made a minister according to the gift of God's grace which was given me by the working of his power. To me, though I am the very least of all the saints, this grace was given, to preach to the Gentiles the unsearchable riches of Christ, and to make all men see what is the plan of the mystery hidden for ages in God who created all things; that through the church the manifold wisdom of God might now be made known to the principalities and powers in the heavenly places. This was according to the eternal purpose which he has realized in Christ Jesus our Lord, in whom we have boldness and confidence of access through our faith in him (Eph. 3:7-12, RSV).

Ideas This Chapter Includes

Church administration leads a church to understand its purpose.

A church's purpose is reflected in its nature and mission.

Church administration tries to enable a church to fulfill its purpose.

Church administration has a unique role in the life of a church. It is a helping role. It is a servant role. It is a ministry. The ministry of administration is to enable the church to become and to do what they can become and do by God's grace.

A church needs and deserves leaders. Those who lead have several areas in which they must give leadership. They must lead a church to:

Clarify its purpose
Determine its objectives
Develop ministry plans
Design organization
Administer human resources
Administer physical resources
Administer financial resources
Provide controls

These functional areas in which church leaders lead make up the scope of administration. These areas are like great land masses on a planet. This book is intended to identify and to explore the planet of church administration, continent by continent. This chapter explores the functional area of *purpose.*

Administration Helps Clarify Purpose

The first task of church administration is to lead a church to understand its purpose. This is a continuing assignment for those who lead a church. Leaders and members need continually to clarify the purpose of church and to keep that purpose before people in and out of the church fellowship.

Ask "Why?"

What is a church? What is not a church? What is church for? What is church not for? Why have church? How do you justify having church? What is its reason for existence? What is its settled determination, the ultimate justification for being? These are the kinds of questions which, when answered, lead to understanding about the purpose of church. Such understanding is indispensible for a church to maximize its ministries. A church which lives and works *on purpose* is much more likely to realize and to fulfill its mission than a church which lives and works *by accident*.

Consider the Founder's Intent

Where should one look for guidance regarding the purpose of church? A good place to begin is to look to the Founder of the church, the Lord of the church, Jesus Christ Himself. What did He have in mind in founding the church? Is there a word from the Lord? Indeed there is!

The Master Teacher was giving His students, the disciples, a "mid-term" examination. Matthew recorded this experience.

> Now when Jesus came into the district of Caesarea Philippi, he asked his disciples, "Who do men say that the Son of man is?" And they said, "Some say John the Baptist, others say Elijah, and others Jeremiah or one of the prophets." He said to them, "But who do you say that I am?" Simon Peter replied, "You are the Christ, the Son of the living God." And Jesus answered him, "Blessed are you, Simon Bar-Jona! For flesh and blood has not revealed this to you, but my Father who is in heaven. And I tell you, you are Peter, and on this rock I will build my church, and the powers of death shall not prevail against it. I will give you the keys of the kingdom of heaven, and whatever you bind on earth shall be bound in heaven, and whatever you loose on earth shall be loosed in heaven (Matt. 16:13-19, RSV).

Here Jesus declared that He would build His church. What did Jesus set out to build? What did He mean when He spoke of the church? Why should Jesus build a church? What is the purpose of church? Surely those who administer a church, as well as those who make up the church, should seek answers to these very important questions.

Examine the Nature of a Church

Perhaps the search for answers to these questions should consider what a church *is*—its *nature;* and what a church is *to do*—its *mission.* Together these insights should help to show more clearly the purpose of church.

Nature refers to essential character.—What church *is*—its *nature*—has to do with its essential character, its distinguishing quality or qualities, its essence. There are numerous concepts of what church is. Some of these concepts are inadequate or incorrect. For instance, some think mainly of a *building* when they hear or say the word *church.* They think of it as a place in a particular location. This is probably the most common perception of church to persons outside a church fellowship, and it is not uncommon to many who are members of a fellowship.

It is easy to see how persons could mistake the building or the place of meeting for the church, in light of the thousands and thousands of buildings which even the members of churches refer to as the church. However, there were numerous churches before there were ever buildings *called* churches. They met in homes, in open places, in borrowed buildings, and in other places. It wasn't until about the third century AD that churches began to have buildings of their own in which to meet. To think of church primarily in terms of a building doesn't get to the basic nature of church. It is an inadequate concept of church.

Sometimes the word *church* is used to refer to *organized Christianity or to a group of churches,* such as *a denomination.* Such use never occurs in the New Testament.[1] *Catholic*

The New Testament does speak of the church as the *body of Christ which includes all of the redeemed of all the ages.*[2] However, at no time has this usage of the term referred to a body of specific persons in a single location at the same point in history. Nor does the "church general" need our administrative attentions. It is the "local chapters" of present-day members of the body of Christ which call for services of administration. This was true in the New Testament references to church.

Nature is seen in biblical expressions.—The Bible records some phrases referring to church which, taken together, provide a rich study of the nature of the church. The apostles Paul and Peter both wrote of the church as people of God. Paul in Galatians 3:29 wrote of "Abraham's offspring" (RSV) and again in 6:16 of "the Israel of God." Peter used an array of terms when he wrote of the church as "a chosen race, a royal priesthood, a holy nation, God's own people" (1 Pet. 2:9, RSV).

Paul wrote of "the church of God" (1 Cor. 1:2; 10:32; 11:22; 2 Cor. 1:1; Gal. 1:13; 1 Tim. 3:5) and of "the churches of God" (1 Cor. 11:16; 1 Thess. 2:14; 2 Thess. 1:4). Gospel writers referred to the church as God's flock (Matt. 26:31; Luke 12:32; also see John 10:16; 21:15,17).

Again, Paul wrote of a new humanity, a "new man" (Eph. 2:14-20) and "a new creation" (Gal. 6:15, RSV). He wrote of the church as the bride of Christ (2 Cor. 11:2-3; Eph. 5:25-32), and so did the writer of Revelation (19:7-9; 21:9).

Paul used several other expressions in referring to the church: "the pillar and bulwark of the truth" (1 Tim. 3:15); "God's field" (1 Cor. 3:9); "God's building" (still talking about people, not structure in 1 Cor 3:9); and "the body of Christ" in numerous references (Rom. 12:4-5; 1 Cor. 12:12-27; Eph. 1:22-23; 2:14-16; 3:3-13; 4:1-16; 5:30; Col. 1:18,24; 2:16-19:3:15).

Mark wrote of the church in terms of a family (3:33-35). John described it as the relationship of branch and vine (John 15:1-8). In his letters John wrote of a *koinonia*, a fellowship (1 John 1:3) and of "children of God" (John 1:11-12 RSV).

What an array of ideas! These biblical portraits indicate that a church is something very special.

Word study on church.—A brief word study of *church* should help to understand more of the nature of church. The English word *church* translates the Greek word *ekklesia*, which means "the called-out ones," or "assembly." It was used prior to the New Testament to designate the assembly of citizens of a self-governing Greek city. "In this sense an *ekklesia* was a local assembly opperating through democratic processes under the laws of the Empire."[3] It was also used in the Greek translation of the Old Testament, the Septuagint, to translate the Hebrew word *qahal,* "referring to the nation of Israel assembled before God and under his direct theocratic rule (Deut. 31:12, congregation; Judg. 21:8, assembly."[4]

The Southern Baptist Convention in session in 1963 adopted a statement called "The Baptist Faith and Message." Although not intended as a creedal statement, "The Baptist Faith and Message" is an important document. It includes a descriptive statement about the church:

> A New Testament church of the Lord Jesus Christ is a local body of baptized believers who are associated by covenant in the faith and fellowship of the gospel, observing the two ordinances of Christ, committed to His Teachings, exercising the gifts, rights, and privileges invested in them by His Word, and seeking to extend the gospel to the ends of the earth.

> This church is an autonomous body, operating through democratic processes under the Lordship of Jesus Christ. In such a congregation members are equally responsible. Its Scriptural officers are pastors and deacons.

> The New Testament speaks also of the church as the body of Christ which includes all of the redeemed of all the ages.

> Matt. 16:15-19; 18:15-20; Acts 2:41-42, 47; 5:11-14; 6:3-6; 13:1-3; 14:23, 27; 15:1-30; 16:5; 20:28; Rom. 1:7; 1 Cor. 1:2; 3:16; 5:4-5; 7:17; 9:13-14; 12; Eph. 1:22-23; 2:19-22; 3:8-11; 21; 5:22-32; Phil. 1:1; Col. 1:18; 1 Tim. 3:1-15; 4:14; 1 Pet. 5:1-4; Rev. 2-3; 21:2-3.[5]

Local church is a colony.—The local church is not interpreted to be the entire kingdom of God, and membership in a church should not be equated with salvation. In the broad sense the kingdom of God is the reign of God in His creation. "The local church is an earthly colony of that kingdom."[6] Writing about salvation, church membership, and the two biblical ideas of church, Hobbs stated:

> Thus while salvation is synonymous with membership in the church general, it is not true with regard to local church membership. Nor is membership in the local church synonymous

with salvation. "Fellowship," not "membership," is the New Testament word for Christian relations in the local church.[7]

Based upon a study of the Bible, you can develop your own understanding of what the nature of the church is to be. In keeping with the priesthood of all believers, this is both the privileges and responsibility of the individual believer. The individual has primary responsibility for what he or she believes and for how those beliefs impact others. If the beliefs of one person cause problems for the church, then the members must determine how they will accomodate themselves to the situation. All should seek to know and to obey the mind of Christ.[8]

An interpretative model helps grasp the nature of church. —It is important to study the church as an idea. It is also helpful to look briefly at the nature of the church from an individual's viewpoint. Church begins with a call to discipleship. Christ calls individuals to discipleship. Many persons might respond to His call in the same time and place, but each one is called individually. This was true when Jesus called those first ones to Himself. This call is recorded in Mark 1:17: "And Jesus said to them, 'Follow me and I will make you become fishers of men' " (RSV). He was calling a pair of brothers, fishermen Peter and Andrew.

What did Jesus have in mind when He called these individuals to discipleship? What did He mean when He invited people to "Follow me"?

Followers keep company with Jesus and one another.—It would seem that He meant for those who would follow Him to come and be in company with Him. Since He invited several persons, it would seem, too, that He intended that those who should follow Him would also keep company with one another. Yet there must have been more. He was not gathering about Him a group of individuals just with the idea of having some introverted fellowship with Him and with one another.

Followers live His way.—"Follow me" suggests much more than fellowship. It was a call to a discipleship which is more than companionship. It was a call to learn from Him, to be His pupil. It was a call to His discipline for life. *It was a call to live life His way in relation to the Father and to others.* It was not a call to a standard of living in some material sense but to a standard for life. The new relationship begins with reconciliation with God and is to be expressed in relationships with others. The Bible has much to say about both of these dimensions.

Followers join Him in the redemptive enterprise.—One significant dimension of what the call to discipleship meant and still means is the latter part of the spoken call: "I will make you become fishers of men." *The call to discipleship integrally means a call to live His way and to join Him in the redemptive enterprise.* So committed was Jesus to our joining Him in the redemptive enterprise that He gave His task to His disciples with the promise of the indwelling Spirit to guide and to empower Him. He also declared:

> Truly, truly, I say to you, he who believes in me will also do the works that I do; and greater works than these will he do, because I go to the Father (John 14:12, RSV).

Surely disciples could not do works greater in *kind* than those done by the Master. Whatever else Jesus might have meant, surely He meant that His disciples are to be faithful in doing the things which would be a blessing to others, the highest blessing being reconciliation to the Father through Christ.

What does the call to discipleship have to do with the nature of the church? *The call to discipleship is the nature of the church, when that call is lived out in its intended way.* An individual disciple is one part of that body, the church. Discipleship involves joining the company of others who are also disciples and working together with Christ to bring persons to God.

Church is a "building" made of people.—Church is built upon the Rock. A church is more than a collection of persons. It is a "building"—not a building made of stones, but a building made of people who are disciples of Jesus Christ.

Jesus came with His disciples into the district of Caesarea Philippi. He asked them who men were saying that He the Son of man is. They mentioned John the Baptist, Elijah, Jeremiah, or one of the prophets.

He said to them, "But who do you say that I am? Simon Peter replied, You are the Christ, the Son of the living God." And Jesus answered him, "Blessed are you, Simon Bar-Jona! For flesh and blood has not revealed this to you, but my Father who is in heaven. And I tell you, you are Peter [Petros], and on this rock [petra] I will build my church, and the powers of death shall not prevail against it. I will give you the keys of the kingdom of heaven, and whatever you bind on earth shall be bound in heaven, and whatever you loose on earth shall be loosed in heaven" (Matt. 16:15-19, RSV).

Hobbs wrote, "A petra was a large ledge rock such as a foundation rock. A petros was a small stone broken off the large stone and partaking of its nature."[9] He continued, "In the Old Testament where 'rock' is used symbolically, it always refers to deity."[10] So, what should one make of this complex passage and of its meaning for the individual and the church? Consider this treatment.

Certainly the foundation of the church is Christ, not Peter or any other mere mortal (1 Cor. 3:11). . . . The writer sees "rock" as referring to Christ. Peter was a *petros,* a small stone partaking of Christ's nature. The church is built upon Christ, the building stones being all who, like Peter, confess Him as "the Christ, the Son of the Living God." (See 1 Pet. 2:5.)[11]

Individuals who respond to Jesus' call to discipleship and confess Him as Lord follow Him and live His way in relation to God and mankind and share with Him in the redemptive enterprise are His church. Each individual is a piece of the rock, the foundation stone of which the church is built. Each has equal opportunity of access to the Father. Each has a share of the privileges. Each has a voice and, when needed, a vote. Not all have equal influence in the body. Such influence usually comes to those who are faithful with the responsibilities or opportunities they have.

Gifts are for enabling the church.—He has supplied certain ones with gifts which are to be used for the good of the body as the church goes about the work of the Kingdom. The gifts are for functional services which are to enable those in the fellowship, to equip them for the work of ministry. There are varieties of gifts, but the same Spirit, same Lord, same God. No part of the body, no member, whatever one's gift may be, is to disdain another or to set oneself over another as though he or she were of a higher order.

Church is a living organism. The individual believer has new life. A person is indwelt by the Spirit from the time of the new birth. One is a "new person" in Christ, part of a new humanity. This new life is different from the old life. The believer is to live as Jesus lived in relation to the Father and to others. Banding together voluntarily under the lordship of Christ, individual believers comprise a church.

There is a sense in which the believers who are banded together to form a church have life in a corporate relationship. They become an entity of life. They take on qualities of an organism. In this instance, an organism is any highly complex thing or structure with parts so integrated that their relationship to one another is governed by their relationship to the whole. This seems to be the concept of the church Paul advocated in 1 Corinthians 12:14*ff.* and Ephesians 4:11*ff.*

Just as Christ is the source of new life in the individual through the Holy Spirit, He is also the source of life and strength of the body of believers—the fellowship we call a church. He directs the life of the organism. He supplies its power, its strength. That is the *nature* of church. That is its essential character, its essence.

Examine the Mission of a Church

Now consider the *mission* of a church. That along with the *nature* of church should help us understand its *purpose*. The noun *mission* means first "a sending forth." It implies that there is some *charge* for which those sent forth are responsible. There is *purpose* to be fulfilled. There is an *errand* to be performed. There is a *commission* to be carried out. All of these elements grow out of the nature of the church. A church does what it does because it is what it is. What is its mission?

To make known the manifold wisdom of God: the gospel. —It is the mission of a church to make known the manifold wisdom of God (Eph. 3:10). The individual who comes to know the manifold wisdom of God, the "plan of the mystery" (v. 9, RSV), can respond in faith, receive Christ, and become a child of God. The people who have already received Christ are to make known the wisdom of God. This wisdom is the gospel, the good news.

Christ gave His church the responsibility of unbinding the gospel, letting it loose in the earth. But with this responsibility comes also the possibility that a church might not unbind the gospel and, by this very default, will bind it. Not all children obey the Father. Consider this comment about Matthew 16:- 19:

> The keys of the kingdom are the gospel which Jesus deposited in his church. If the church binds it on earth by not proclaiming it, heaven has already decreed that there is no other way whereby men may be saved and enter into the kingdom of heaven. But if the church looses the gospel on earth by proclaiming it, heaven has already decreed that men will hear it, some will believe it, and those who do will be saved or enter into the kingdom of heaven. It is a privilege and a tremendous responsibility![12]

It is essential to the nature of the church that its members be faithful in proclaiming the gospel. It is the only hope of salvation for mankind. As Peter declared, "There is salvation in no one else, for there is no other name under heaven given among men by which we must be saved" (Acts 4:12, RSV).

A church is a fellowship of disciples making known to all the gospel of Jesus Christ. Its mission is not to be a fellowship. That is its nature. It is a fellowship. Its mission is to make the gospel known. It is a fellowship on mission.

SBC curriculum and program leaders work with a statement of a church's mission.—Designers of Southern Baptist Convention (SBC) curriculum materials and program designs have done extensive work over recent years in proposing accurate and practical answers to questions regarding the essential functions of a church on mission. They are working with this statement of a church's mission as their premise:

> The mission of a church, composed of baptized believers who share a personal commitment to Jesus Christ as Savior and Lord, is to be a redemptive body in Christ, through the power of the Holy Spirit, growing toward Christian maturity through

worship, proclamation and witness, nurture and education, and ministry to the whole world that God's purpose may be achieved.[13]

Using this statement of a church's mission, we shall focus on the functions of a church as valid expressions of what a church does as it carries out its mission. *A function is a basic activity natural to, characteristic of, and essential to the life of an organism.* What are the functions of a church? They are four.

Worship is the foundational function of a church.—Worship is a basic activity of a church. It is an individual "encountering God in experiences that deepen a Christian's faith and strengthen his service."[14] It is a natural expression of one's relationship to God. No one should be surprised to find a believer worshiping. It is an act and an attitude which characterizes believers. It is essential to the life of the church. Without worship, frequently and regularly, the organism cannot long perform its other functions. Worship supports proclamation, protective nurture, maturing education, and ministry to others that is more than mere humanism.

Corporate worship, with believers gathering together and experiencing encounter with God as a body of His children, is imperative (Heb. 10:25). It is a beginning point and a melding point for a church with regard to its development into a genuine fellowship. Moreover, those who comprise a church must also experience worship individually, apart from corporate occasions. These times of one-to-one encounter sustain the individual's identity as an individual disciple and contribute strength to his relationship to the others when they come together for worship or for other purposes. Neither corporate worship, individual worship, nor both kinds together comprise the totality of one's responsibility to God or His church. A body of believers whose members only worship cannot be a complete church. Conversely, to whatever extent the members neglect worship, to that extent they limit the total ministry of their church. Worship provides the basis for a fellowship on mission. It gives the message and the motive for all the other functions of a church.

Proclaim and witness comprise a vital function.—Proclaim

and *witness* comprise another basic function of a church. It is natural that disciples of Jesus Christ should tell others what they themselves have seen and heard, what they have experienced with Christ. It is characteristic of one who has had a vital experience to want to share the Word with others in order that they might also experience such joy and relatedness. It is essential that the faithful proclaim and witness, both for what it does for those who proclaim and for those who hear. It is life-extending for the body.

Verbal proclaiming and verbal witnessing, both oral and written, are vital. One who has encountered Christ and experienced salvation has something to tell! But no amount of telling, even without a magnificent conversion experience, can adequately compensate for a careless life-style which seems to belie the care of Christ for persons which a believer's life should reflect. One who runs roughshod over others as though they were less than persons for who Christ lived, died, and rose to live again cannot proclaim or witness with credibility. Also, not all of the verbal proclaiming has to fall into one set pattern. Not every disciple feels free to be as bold or as confrontational as to some others. Certainly these less bold ones should not be shamed or ridiculed by fellow disciples. All need to develop some ways of verbally proclaiming or witnessing but in ways which are natural to their own personalities. In any case, the witness of one's life and behavior might be the most effective word spoken.

A church must proclaim and witness. To whatever extent it does, a church can expect increased vitality and new life—indeed new lives—to be added to the body. To whatever extent a church neglects to proclaim and witness, to that extent it can expect to suffer loss of vitality and the absence of new life. Proclaiming and witnessing are major means of making known the gospel, the manifold wisdom of God.

Nurture and educate make up an indispensable function. —It is a basic function of a church to *nurture* and *educate*. It is natural for a church to "nourish, modify, and develop individuals within a fellowship."[15] This is one expression of concern for persons and their needs. It is natural for a church to provide maturing and growing persons in knowledge, wisdom, moral righteousness, and performance. None should be surprised to find a church engaged in activities to help persons in these ways. Rather, it should characterize a church to be found faithfully working at nurture and education.

A church must engage its members in regular and frequent nurturing and educating experiences. There is no amount of nurture or education which can substitute for the conscious submission of one's will to the lordship of Christ for salvation. Nor can nurture and education supplant worship, proclamation and witness, or ministry. But to fail to nurture and educate is to risk aborting the discipling cycle.

It is imperative that a church nurture and educate. The God of all truth intends for His truth to be made known for the good of His creation as they begin and continue the disciple life. Nurture and education are ways this can be done.

Ministry is a function every church needs.—To minister is a basic activity of a church. To minister is to do things needful or helpful—to aid persons both in and out of its fellowship. Distinctively Christian ministering, such as a church renders, is that which is done in the name of Christ, through His power, in His Spirit, and for His glory. Just as those who comprise a church are emulating Christ when they worship, proclaim, and educate, so they emulate Him when they minister to those in need. And while any church might hope that those to whom they minister would accept their highest expression of loving concern—the gospel of Christ for their salvation—such acceptance is not a condition for the help to be given. Individually and collectively, the church actively ministers to the spiritual, mental, and physical needs of persons.

Ministry is largely made up of voluntary acts, those which a church consciously chooses to do to help persons because the people of the church love God, and they love and care for others as they care for themselves. Some sincere persons might mistake the channel of ministry as the way to earn salvation. This is regrettable, because Christian ministering comes from one who is first a Christian.

Salvation is something given, not earned. Just as one cannot be educated into the Kingdom, neither can one work one's way in by helping people. But there is a serious error at the other end of this spectrum. There are many who declare themselves Christians, who will freely proclaim and witness and who will study and learn, but never minister beyond the verbal. These Christians need encouragement toward a fuller participation in the life of the church. To fail to minister is to risk spiritual decay. Members of the fellowship—the church—need to minister both to help others in need and to help themselves develop as disciples.

A church on mission is a fellowship on mission. One can tell when this is the case because a church will be doing with some regularity and balance of emphasis those natural, characteristic, essential activities which are the functions of a church: worship, proclaim and witness, nurture and educate, and minister.[16]

What, then, is the *purpose* of church? There might be many ways to say it with accuracy. Nolan Howington wrote that the purpose of a church is "to carry out the will of Christ in the world, to proclaim and apply his gospel."[17] This is clear and simple. In my opinion, it is accurate.

Author's statement of purpose of church.—Another way of stating the purpose of church is not as easily said but reflects the church's nature and mission in terms of this presentation. *The purpose of church is to be a fellowship of persons who have received Christ and who are attempting obediently to live the way of Christ and to work faithfully with Him to bring others to God.*

Different people probably would state the purpose of church in different ways. The point to keep in mind is that leaders and members of a church need to have a consensus understanding about the purpose of church which serves as a touchstone, a rallying point, and a reference point for guidance in all they undertake to do as a church. *It is an administrative responsibility to lead a church in this understanding, and to keep it before the leaders and members as together they try to do the work of a church.*

Administration Enables a Church to Be a Church

It is the work of administration to enable a church to be a church on purpose and to do the work of a church. How does administration relate to a church in ways compatible with this concept? That is what this book is about.

Administrative Leaders Help Members
Clarify Purpose and to Act Upon it

Some persons have gifts of administration. Paul, especially, wrote of these gifts. He included administrators in his listing of gifts in 1 Corinthians 12:28 and in other places. He said of the gifts in Ephesians 4:12 that they were given "for the immediate equipment of the Children of God for the work of service" (Williams). Administration is an enabling gift. As believers come together and form a church, administration enables the members to identify and clarify their purpose.

In today's churches, it might be the Church Council or the long-range planning committee of a church which leads in the development of purpose. In some churches, a special committee for this purpose might be called into being. In any event, there needs to be widespread involvement of members in the process of developing a statement of purpose. The church should ratify the final statement of purpose. It should be part of a church's documents, such as its constitution and bylaws. But it must not remain locked in some obscure place only to be discovered by some diligent historian in the future.

Purpose Permeates Church Objectives

The undertaking of purpose should permeate the thinking of those who determine a church's objectives. Objectives are those statements that reflect in somewhat ultimate terms what kind of church the members of the fellowship believe God wants the church to become. These statements of objectives verbalize directions in which the energies of a church are to be focused in light of theological and philosophical insights as to what God wants the church to be. In the next chapter we will deal in detail with leading a church to minister by objectives.

Purpose and Objectives Guide in Ministry Planning

Purpose and objectives provide the ideological backdrop against which a church develops its program—its plans for ministry. A church's program is what the church does intentionally as an expression of its awareness of and commitment to meeting the needs of persons in light of its purpose and objectives. Chapter four is the one in which we consider developing a church ministry plan. In it we shall see that what a church does in its program must be evaluated by its purpose and objectives. The program must make some contribution to moving a church toward fulfillment of its objectives and realization of its purpose.

Program (Ministry Plan) Determines Organization

A church's purpose, objectives, and program speak to its design of organization. Organization in a church involves the patterns for relating persons to one another to accomplish the program, which in turn helps move a church toward its objectives in light of its purpose. There is a definite sequence of the functional areas of administration. Thus far we have mentioned purpose, objectives, program, and organization.

Resources and Controls Are Geared to Program, Objectives, and Purpose

Clarity of purpose helps a church to maximize its resources: human, physical, and financial. The administration of these vital areas is the subject of subsequent chapters. And in these and all other areas of a church's life work, administration helps to provide effective controls—guidance which helps to assure that what is done is closely approximate to what was intended. This, too, is the subject of a later chapter.

Church administration and the purpose of church are very closely interrelated. Good administration begins with a church's purpose and tries to help a church to realize its purpose. Jesus loved the church and gave Himself for it. Good church administration enables those of the fellowship to do the same.

Summary

Church administration exists to enable a church. The first task of church administration is to help a church clarify its purpose. As a church seeks to clarify its purpose, it should consider the intent of the Lord of the church. It should examine the nature and mission of a church.

The nature of a church is found in its unique fellowship. Its mission is to make the gospel known in all its fullness. Certain essential functions characterize the life of a church on mission: worship, proclamation and witness, nurture and education, and ministry.

The purpose of church is to be a fellowship of persons who have received Christ, and who are attempting obediently to live the way of Christ and to work faithfully with Him to bring others to God. It is an administrative responsibility to lead a church to understand its purpose, and to keep it before the leaders and members as together they try to do the work of a church. A church's program, organization, human resources, physical resources, financial resources, and controls should grow out of and contribute to fulfilling its purpose.

Learning Activity Suggestions

1. Interview five members of one church, one at a time, apart from one another, asking them to tell you in a sentence or two what they think is the purpose of their church. Write down these statements. Compare them with the statements of purpose suggested in this chapter.

2. Review the Scriptures and other literature you can find on the purpose of the church. Write your own statement of the purpose of church. Explain the components of your statement in five hundred words or less.

3. Prepare a three-to-five-minute speech relating church administration to the purpose of a church.

Notes

1. Herschel H. Hobbs, *The Baptist Faith and Message* (Nashville: Convention Press, 1971), p. 75.

2. Ibid., p. 74.

3. Ibid., p. 75.

4. Ibid.

5. Ibid., p. 74.

6. Ibid., p. 79.

7. Ibid., p. 80.

8. Charles A. Tidwell, *Educational Ministry of a Church* (Nashville: Broadman Press, 1982), pp. 88-90.

9. Hobbs. p. 76.

10. Ibid.

11. Ibid.

12. Ibid., p. 78.

13. Howard P. Colson and Raymond M. Rigdon, *Understanding Your Church's Curriculum,* revised edition (Nashville: Broadman Press, 1981), p. 45.

14. Reginald M. McDonough, comp., *A Church on Mission* (Nashville: Convention Press, 1980), p. 17.

15. Ibid., p. 18.

16. Tidwell, pp. 90-95.

17. Nolan Howington, "Church Base Design Revision," (unpublished paper, July 20, 1978), p. 9.

3
Ministering by Objectives

You are the salt of the earth. . . . You are the light of the world (Matt. 5:13-14, RSV).

But you shall receive power when the Holy Spirit has come upon you; and you shall be my witnesses in Jerusalem and in all Judea and Samaria and to the end of the earth (Acts 1:8, RSV).

And Jesus came and said to them, "All authority in heaven and on earth has been given to me. Go therefore and make disciples of all nations, baptizing them in the name of the Father and of the Son and of the Holy Spirit, teaching them to observe all that I have commanded you; and lo, I am with you always, to the close of the age" (Matt. 28:18-20, RSV).

Ideas This Chapter Includes

A definition of objectives

Some benefits of objectives in the church

A sample set of objectives and the process a church used to develop them

How to use objectives, once developed

Administration and Objectives

Good administration begins with a church's *purpose* and tries to help the church to realize its purpose. Jesus loved the church and gave Himself for it. Good church administration enables those of the fellowship to give themselves in service of the church.

A church's statement of purpose probably will be a single

statement that attempts to include or allow for the fulfillment of all the nature and mission of a church. This statement is like an umbrella which covers the full scope of the body. It is a very idealistic, lofty concept. It is a good place to begin in leadership but not a good place to stop. The purpose must be "imagineered" from the "softy-lofty" to the "nitty-gritty" of everyday life and translated into ministry plans for which there must be organization, resources, and controls.

Many churches find it helpful to determine *objectives* which serve as practical guides for ministry planning. Objectives bring the purpose concept one step nearer to where the action begins as they move toward fulfilling their purpose.

Definition of Objectives

Writing of educational objectives, Paul H. Vieth stated:

An objective is a statement of a result consciously accepted as a desired outcome of a given process. It springs from the recognition that there are alternative consequences which may follow from acting in given situations in different ways. It signifies that an activity has been raised to the level of consciousness, where the desired outcome may enter as a factor in controlling the possible ways of responding to given situations. An objective introduces foresight into a process and uses the anticipated outcome in directing that process.[1]

W. L. Howse described objectives as:

simple statements of what we're trying in our work to bring about. They are continuing aims toward which we direct our efforts. Objectives indicate our choices as to the essential things for which we exist and toward which we strive.[2]

An objective is used by many in educational technology and in other disciplines as an immediate result or outcome. In church administration, especially in the churches and institutions of the Southern Baptist Convention, an objective is seen as an end adopted as a desired result toward which an entity or an individual functions. It expresses some maximum stage beyond which further progress is unlikely. In these settings, a goal is used to identify an immediate result or outcome.

As used in church leadership, *objectives are statements of ultimate ends toward which a church aims its energies.* They are statements of a church's understanding of the *kind* of church God wants them to *be.* They identify outcomes in areas of a church's timeless intention to act. They are best stated in terms of *being* rather than *acting* or *doing.* People who have clear concepts of who they are and of who they are becoming generally reflect these concepts of identity in their actions. These concepts we call *objectives.*

Is it worth the time and effort for a church to consider where it might be if it arrived at the place it is now headed? Why should churches struggle with formulating objectives? Don't church leaders and members know what the church is trying to accomplish? What can objectives do for a church? We shall look at some benefits of objectives for a church.

Objectives Reflect Values

Objectives tell what is important to a church. Jesus said, "You shall be my witnesses," as he was about to ascend. In other instances He said His followers should be salt and light. He also said, "Do not be like them," referring to hypocrites and those who talk in empty phrases. It should help a church to know who it is and what it values as a church.

A church adopted this statement as one of its objectives: "Our objective is to be witnesses for Christ both in this community and throughout the world." This church declared that being witnesses for Christ both at home and abroad is an imperative value. It implied that being witnesses for Christ is more important than some other things a church might be. A church whose members really believe such an objective is likely to do more than they otherwise would about being witnesses for Christ.

Objectives Direct Your Efforts

Objectives function like the North Star in navigation. They enable a church to check its bearing and to move with assurance in the direction it feels God wants it to move.

Some churches seem to be static. They apparently are not moving. They need a sense of direction. Objectives can give direction to such churches.

Some churches seem to be moving in all directions. There might be a lot of activity, but not much progress. Members might seem thrilled by the commotion. Some might be ill with motion sickness. They are moving, but not with unity. They are marching, but with broken steps. Objectives can help bring order and direction to a church that seems to be moving in all directions.

Some churches are moving backward. They are losing ground. They might be wondering why. For those who wonder, there is hope if they search for and find their direction. Objectives can help a backward-moving church by giving them clear objectives toward which they should work.

Churches which commit themselves firmly and realistically to an objective like "being witnesses for Christ both in this community and throughout the world" have a positive direction in which to move. Such churches can scarcely be static, unguided, or backward. Objectives give direction to their efforts.

Objectives Are Standards for Selecting Means

Objectives are *ends* which should determine what *means* a church will choose and plan to do. Activities are not ends but are means to help accomplish ends. Organizations should not be ends but means. Physical resources and money are not ends; they are means. When means are mistaken for ends, you have "end-means inversion." You have activities for activities' sake. You have organizations whether you need them or not. You have buildings which are largely unused. Leaders feel compelled to talk often of the need for money but never seem to have enough, because the end for which it goes it not seen as worthy.

For each proposal in church planning, questions like these should help: (1) Is this in character with our church objectives? (2) Would this help move us toward our objectives? (3) Are there other choices that might do more to move us toward our objectives?

A church needs some standards, some criteria for deciding what means it will use to fulfill its purpose as a church. Objectives can serve as standards against which to check the means a church might consider. Good objectives can help a church put first things first.

From time to time as church leaders consider means and try to make good decisions about them, they might find that what is being considered doesn't seem to relate to any of the church's stated objectives. In this case, leaders should review the objectives to see if they are as broad as they should be. If not, they should propose revising them to meet the needs. If they are already inadequate, they should acknowledge this fact and move on to the next consideration.

A church is unwise to engage in any activity, change any organization, modify physical resources, or spend any money that does not meet the test of contributing to its objectives. The church must be the church. The church must do the work of the church. To this end, a church is right to leave undone or to leave for other organizations and groups that which is out of character with its purpose and objectives. With limited time, energies, physical, and financial resources, a church must be the best steward of these means with God's help. Objectives are standards for selecting means.

Objectives Motivate People

One of the concerns in leadership is how to motivate people to do what needs to be done. There is a lot that is not known about how to motivate people. But one thing that *is* known is that there is a direct correlation between the perceived worthiness of a cause and the willingness of persons to support that cause. A church has the most worthy of causes! Why don't people just fall all over themselves in support of the cause? One reason is that leaders have not helped them to clearly perceive the extreme worthiness of the cause. They help express what it is to which leaders are calling people. They communicate worthy outcomes for which every child of God would want to strive. Good objectives call forth increased participation from believers.

Programs, as important as they are, do not offer the highest motivational possibilities. Organizational loyalty is not the ultimate for which people are willing to give themselves. Buildings and other physical resources do not give highest expression to the cause. Appeals for money become irritating when they are not clearly tied to worthy outcomes or obligations. Motivational possibilities of the highest order lie in calling people to the worthy purpose of the church and to the long-term objectives which will lead the church to fulfill its purpose.

There are other considerations which add to a person's willingness to participate in working toward church objectives. One consideration is that they should share in determining what the objectives will be.

Leaders might withdraw from the busy lives they lead long enough to write some beautiful statements of objectives. They could have copies made, pass them out at the door on church business meeting night, and persuade those present to vote in favor of the statements. What would they have accomplished? Just about what they have so often accomplished when they have tried to lead people in this fashion: their approval for the leaders to go ahead and try to do the job, or their pledge not to try to keep the leaders from going ahead. The vote of approval gained in such a manner usually means no more than, "It's OK with us, if that's the way you want to do it."

A *meaningful* vote of support not only means "We are definitely in favor," but also "Count on us for whatever it takes to get the job done!" People who have a real part in helping to shape the objectives are more likely to be motivated to give their support to help accomplish the objectives.

Certainly it helps, too, if people understand and agree with the objectives. This can be accomplished by participation initially in formulating objectives and in good communication of objectives for as long as they are used to lead the church. Look, for example, at the objective we have referred to already— "Our objectives is to be witnesses for Christ both in this community and throughout the world." This should be an excellent statement upon which to base promotional appeals for people to take part in witnessing programs, in Sunday School outreach visitation, and even in mission support. Leaders could convey that participation in these programs is more than just doing good things to be doing good things. They could communicate "We are trying as best we know how to be witnesses for Christ to a world of people who desperately need Him! Here's how you can have a part in this most worthy cause! Here's how you can give real expression to your profession of discipleship. Jesus called us to join Him in the redemptive enterprise. Here's a way for you to do just that!"

Children of God—people who have received Christ—do respond to good objectives which they have helped to formulate, which they understand, and with which they agree. They identify with such objectives personally. People are least interested when called upon to work toward objectives someone else has determined.

One Church's Experience

Macedonia Baptist Church, a rural church, was in a pilot project in which church plans were being developed for seven to ten years into the future. Their pastor was a good, older man with no seminary training, but with a college education and good ministry experience. One of the things he led the church to do was to develop some good objectives. In the process of doing this, he preached a series of sermons on the biblical purpose and objectives of a church. The church scheduled and conducted a study unit in Church Training on the nature and functions of a church. Special committees did extensive studies of the community outside the church membership and discovered what schools, roads, industry, law enforcement, demographics, and other significant factors were expected to be like in their community in the coming decade. They studied their church, its location in relation to other factors, the composition of its members, their strengths and weaknesses. Out of all this they developed some good objectives.

Then they set goals growing out of these objectives. They set goals for year one, year two, year three, and so on through year ten. They developed strategies and action plans for reaching the goals. All of the mechanics for fulfilling their purpose as a church by moving toward their objectives came to be more than mere mechanics. They became parts of a worthy cause.

At the end of year one of the implementation of their plan, they had a problem. It was, "What do we do now that we've reached the goals for year two at the end of the first year?"

They had accomplished two years' work in a single year! That is motivation! Their pastor said, "We had revival in our church as we studied what the Bible says a church should be and do and as we discovered our community needs." Their members frequently expressed excitement to one another about being part of such a fellowship. Objectives will motivate people!

Objectives Will Measure Results

Just as a church uses objectives as criteria or standards for selecting means, it also evaluates results by reflecting upon the ways the chosen means contributed to moving the church toward its objectives. The church chose at some point in planning to conduct certain events. Once conducted, leaders should ask candidly, did these events do for us what we hoped they would do? If so, why? If not, why not? What are the lessons we should learn from these experiences which would help us to do better in the future? What other events might offer promise of greater return on our investment of resources? These and other questions should help a church measure its results in the light of its objectives.

Some Questions Remain

Now that we have shown some of what objectives can do for a church, let's go back to some of the earlier questions. The question was asked, "Don't leaders and members know what the church is trying to accomplish?" The answer is a qualified yes. But without objectives or something very much like objectives in function, there is probably as much variety of opinion about what the church is trying to accomplish as there are members of the church. Each member has some opinion about what the church is trying to accomplish. It's a little like a minister's job description. Every one of the members has some ideas about what the minister should be doing. Some have very vague notions. Some have fairly adequate ideas. Still other probably have very detailed expectations of which the minister has no knowledge.

The beauty of having definite objectives which are appropriately developed and approved is the probability of consensus, of understanding among the leaders and members regarding the directions the church is trying to go. Such consensus provides a setting conducive to leading the church to advance, to make more progress. And all of this can result in more effectiveness with more efficient use of resources.

Many believe God expects us to use the gifts He has given us—including the gift of good administration—to bring people to God through Jesus Christ. Objectives are a significant part of good administration.

Why should a church struggle with formulating objectives? Because they are useful tools in helping to lead the church to fulfill its purpose. And, even in the process of determining objectives and keeping them before the people, leaders will discover there are growth and development opportunity and experience for all who are a part of the process.

Sample Objectives

Is it worth the time and effort to get the church to determine and approve and use objectives? The short answer is yes. Would you think it worth the effort and time if you could lead your church to determine objectives like these, and commit themselves to work toward them?

1. Our objective is to be a covenant fellowship of Christians filled with the Holy Spirit.
2. Our objective is to be a worshiping fellowship in which God encounters persons.
3. Our objective is to be witnesses for Christ both in this community and throughout the world.
4. Our objective is to be a fellowship of maturing Christians whose learning results in responsible living.
5. Our objective is to be a church that unselfishly ministers to persons in the community in Jesus' name.

Ministry Possibilities in Objectives

Could you see yourself working with your people to plan and conduct continuing ministries, projects, and other events to help move your church toward some of these objectives? Look at objective 4. In a time when so many think religious education is complete when a person learns the main facts of the faith, wouldn't it be worthwhile to help people develop attitudes, feelings, and appreciations compatible with the facts of the faith? And better still, wouldn't the Lord be pleased if more of us let what we learn factually result in responsible Christian living?

Certainly it is vitally important to learn the cognitive facts of the Bible. That is one end of the educational experience. But it is the *front* end, not the stopping place. Likewise, conversion is one end of the Christian experience. We must go on from there to become faithful and obedient disciples, reproducing our experience of faith in others. That is Christian education that *is* Christian. That is worth whatever time and energy it takes!

How Objectives Come to Be

What energy and time *does* it take to lead a church to determine and begin to use objectives like those we have seen? These came from a church whose leaders and members were involved over a period of some four to six months just developing these statements and their supporting explanations. Let's recount their experience.

The pastor attended a seminar where he caught the vision of what objectives could do for his church. Then he took a couple of days away from the church, went to a quiet retreat, wrote these objectives, presented them for adoption at the next church business meeting, and that was it. No, no, no! It didn't happen that way. That's the *old* way. Forget that!

Role of the pastor.—The pastor did attend a seminar where he caught the vision of what objectives could do for his church. There he was cautioned *not* to try to write the objectives himself. He was instructed in the values of having leaders and members involved as much as possible in the process. This way they could identify with the product of their labors. They could have a growth experience in the process. They could come to feel a deep commitment to these objectives, and to convey their feelings authentically to others. To have one person do this by himself would produce no better effect than that of securing gummed labels with the church covenant printed on one side and sticking them in the church hymnals. That is not the way!

Role of the Church Council.—Next, the pastor presented the challenge to the Church Council to lead in writing the church objectives. This group, with the pastor as chairperson, was made up of the heads of each church program organization (the Sunday School director, Church Training director, Woman's Missionary Union director, Brotherhood director, minister of music, and chairman of the deacons). These were busy people. Some of them were employed in full-time jobs. They had to find time when they could work together. They settled on a series of Saturdays, from ten o'clock until two. They brought their Bibles, other helpful books, sack lunches, and worked for five or six sessions before they got a first draft.

For each statement of objective they wrote three or four brief paragraphs of explanation, giving what they meant by the statement, some Scripture references which related to it, some indicators of possible implications in the church's ministries, some other published resources related to the statement, and whatever else they thought might help those who had not shared in the drafting as they studied and discussed the objectives.

Role of church members.—The Church Council did several things to get church members' input. They had the directors of Sunday School departments of the youth and adult divisions distribute copies for discussion in their departmental periods from two to four Sunday mornings. Suggestions, criticisms, questions were noted by a designated person, and passed along to the Church Council for consideration. During these same Sundays, the youth and adult Church Training groups studied the objectives, looked up the supporting Scripture references and other materials, and had a person serve as recorder for the group to pass along to the Church Council their reactions. With this kind of response, the Church Council made another draft.

This latter copy was shared with all church members for their study and discussion. Two Wednesday night prayer meeting periods were scheduled and devoted to studying and discussing the proposed objectives. Further changes came from these meetings.

Adopted by church vote in the major worship service.—Finally, a Sunday morning worship service was given to a presentation and discussion of the entire set of statements. At the end of this service, the church was asked to vote their approval of the document. This they did enthusiastically! And with this approval came the directive that these objectives become the guidelines for the Church Council and all other church planning groups as they planned and led the church in ministry. God has blessed that church through this experience. People have reached for Christ and for church membership and others have been witnessed and ministered to.

What to do with objectives after adoption.—That's not all there is to leading a church to minister by objectives. There are times in the Church Council's annual planning when the objectives must be reviewed and possibly revised with church approval. New church members need to have opportunity for study, discussion, and understanding of these objectives to which their church is committed. Prospective staff members should be fully apprised of the church's present objectives. No doubt, leaders will find other ways for church objectives to contribute to making a church more effective and more efficient as the church seeks to fulfill its purpose.

Summary

Good administration begins with purpose and moves next to objectives. Objectives bring the purpose concept one step nearer to where the action begins in the work of a church. Objectives are defined in terms of ultimate results rather than immediate goals.

Objectives reflect values. They direct efforts. They are standards for selecting means. They motivate people. They measure results. Goals, strategies, and action plans come after objectives in planning the work of a church.

One church developed a fine set of objectives with their pastor's leadership. Working through the church council, church leaders and members participated in the process over a period of several months. Eventually the church adopted the objectives, and they became the guidelines for developing that church's ministry plans.

After adopting objectives, the Church Council should lead in reviewing objectives periodically, at least annually. Objectives should be presented to new church members, to prospective church staff members, and to the general membership as the ministries of the church are advanced. Objectives are worth the time required to develop them in a church.

Learning Activity Suggestions

1. Write a statement of church objectives in each of the large areas of the life and work of a church as you see these areas. Try to think in terms of being rather than doing. Begin each statement like this: "Our objective is to be a church . . ."

2. Functions of a church have been identified as worship, proclamation and witness, nurture and education, and ministry. Write an objective in one or more of these functions and list at least three kinds of actions which a church might plan to engage in as they implement the objective(s).

3. Write the basic steps your church might use to determine its objectives. Who would lead in the process? How would you get member involvement, and at what points in the process? How would you get the objectives before the whole church? What would you do with the objectives, once approved?

Notes

1. Paul H. Vieth, *Objectives in Religious Education,* (New York: Harper and Brothers 1930), pp. 18-19.
2. W. L. Howse, comments in a seminar on church administration, 1963.

4
Developing Church Ministry Plans

Truly, truly, I say to you, he who believes in me will also do the works that I do; and greater works than these will he do, because I go to the Father (John 14:12, RSV).

But some will say, "You have faith and I have works." Show me your faith apart from your works, and I by my works will show you my faith (Jas. 2:18, RSV).

We need to remind ourselves that to administer is simply to find the best ways and means of ministering. The end of the church's ministry is the reaching of people, the teaching of people, the winning of people, the enlistment and utilization of people, the development of people, the preaching of the Word of God, the inspiration that people need in a day like ours, and the mission of the church in its great missionary undertakings. These are the ends, but we need effective means. In our day, when effective means are used in all other aspects of life, it would be disastrous for us to fail to use adequate means.[1]

Ideas This Chapter Includes

Values of church planning

Who does the planning

How leaders go about planning

Major types of planning

Key principles of planning

A format for planning

A church is a fellowship of persons who have received Christ. They are attempting obediently to live the way of Christ. They are attempting faithfully to work with Him to bring others to God. The purpose of church is to be the design of relationships for this fellowship.

How can a church move toward realizing its purpose? How can those of the fellowship we call church progress from where they are to where they think God wants them to be? How can a church live His way more obediently? How can a church work more faithfully with Him to bring others to God? How can a church truly *be* the church of the living God? This is the ministry of a church.

Work Plans of a Church

In other chapters we have seen how important it is for a church to clarify its purpose and determine its objectives. We have identified a church's purpose and objectives as the great ends toward which a church should work. They are the "softly-lofty" areas of church administration. They represent a church's ideals, its guiding lights. They are vitally important. But these lofty ideas and ideals must be translated into specific plans in order to have the most value. The "softly-lofty" must come in contact with the "nitty-gritty"—the everyday world in which we live. That is what a church ministry plan—a church program—should do for a church. It should help a church to do what it should do to move toward its objectives and its purpose. That is what this chapter is about.

Careful study of this chapter should help you to grow in your knowledge of what is involved in developing a church ministry plan. You should also be better able to do a more effective job of leading your church to plan its ministries.

Imagine You Are Planning a Trip

Think for a moment about some dream trip you have made or would like to make. Why should you make this trip? What is your destination? In what direction are you thinking of going? What are the points along the way through which you will pass? What are some of the experiences you expect to have on this trip? Do you expect to have others go with you? Who are they? How many? How will you travel? Who will drive? Who will make the necessary arrangements for transportation, lodging, food, and other items? What help do those who have these responsibilities need? Who will supply it? How will you pay for this trip? When will you leave? When will you return?

A Good Plan Is Effective and Efficient

You could add numerous other questions as you think of making a dream trip. Your questions and the answers to them could be called a *plan.* Your plan could be as simple or as complex as you choose. If the plan enables you to go where you want to go with maximum effectiveness and efficiency, it is a good plan. Your trip could be all you hoped it would be.

A church should be on the move. It should be trying to become what God wants it to become. In this sense it is on a trip. There needs to be a *plan* for this trip. Questions about why, where, who, when, how how many, how well, at what expense, and other such questions should be asked and answered as part of the church's plan. This plan is more than just a trip plan—it is a plan for ministry. Some call it the church's program.

A Program Is What You Do

A church program is what you do as an expression of your awareness of and commitment to the church's purpose and objectives. It should be planned in relation to the needs of persons, both in and out of the fellowship. It is what a church does to be obedient to Christ in trying to live His way and to be faithful in working with Him to bring persons to God.

The Church Calendar Is the Map

The visible map for this trip is the church calendar of ministries—the church calendar. Admittedly, there is much more ministry going on in most churches than is placed on the church calendar. There should always be those ministries of spontaneous response of individuals and groups, even the whole church, to the needs of persons. But no church should just sit back and wait for its ministry to happen by accident. The church has a commission. The church has His command

and His gifts. A church must seek His guidance and use His gifts intentionally in ministry.

The Ability to Plan Is a Gift of God

One of the good gifts of God is the capacity to anticipate the future, and to decide, under His will, what we intend to do in that future. That is an implication of James 4:13-17, which concludes by saying, "Whoever know what is right to do and fails to do it, for him it is sin" (RSV). We are made in His image. We have personality. We have potential for eternity. We have the capacity for moral discernment. We have the ability, like Him on a limited scale, to plan—to think in the future tense. What animals can do by instinct, people can do by intent. Whoever fails to do it, for him it is sin.

Avoid Presumptuous Planning

To be sure, people must not be presumptuous in planning. The Bible has much to say about presumptuous planning, and all of it is condemned. But to fail to plan so as not to be presumptuous is not of God. To refuse to plan and then pretend that this refusal is an expression of faith in His power to accomplish His will and way is a cop-out. From the human standpoint, to fail to plan is to plan to fail. People don't control God by their plans, but they do limit His control by not planning.

Values of Planning

A person might ask, "What value is it to plan ministries? What are some benefits of planning versus not planning?" Let's mention several values of planning.

Planning Leads to Progress

Planned ministries can lead to progress instead of mere repetition. It can help a church move toward its objectives, and not just go round and round doing all the same things every year for no better reason than that it is time again to do them. There are some things which need to be done repeatedly, seasonally, year in and year out. But there are some other things waiting to be done which will not be accomplished without planning. Planning can help make those repeated ministries take on more appeal and meaning for more people.

Planning Builds Continuity

Planned ministries can help build in continuity in the church's program. There is so much fragmentation, so much discontinuity in so much of life! Many of the ministries of a church can be planned and conducted in such a way as to have both progress and continuity which people need. Here we are not advocating stagnation but stability. For example, a church needs to plan for continuing ministries in education—Bible teaching and learning, membership training, leader training, missions education, and others. These ministries need as their main "diet" to follow continuing curriculum plans. Temporary, short-term curriculum should only be supplementary, not the main course. Otherwise you are always starting and stopping, like repeatedly cranking your car in the driveway and never getting out to the street.

Planning Reflects Unity

Well-planned church ministries reflect unity. There is a variety of gifts. But these gifts are to be exercised and used in ways which are complementary, not competitive. Our diversity of gifts can be magnified in power when expressed in planned unity—not uniformity—*unity!*

The various tasks of a church need to be planned to be supportive of one another. For example, those who are responsible for leading a church to proclaim the gospel to believers and unbelievers can have better results if those responsible for training people to witness are planning and working intentionally to complement the proclaiming task.

Planning Develops Leaders and Members and Brings Others to Christ

Properly planned and conducted ministries develop leaders and members, and bring others to Him. While working together in planning, leaders get to know and to love one another more. It is in planning, as in praying, that we share our burdens, our hearts' desires for the fellowship and for the lost. As a result, members have better experiences and are developed. And most would agree that more of the lost are won to Christ through intentional witnessing than are won by accident.

Leaders in Planning

The Pastor

Who should lead in developing a church's ministry plans—its program? The pastor has the primary individual responsibility, privilege, and sometimes burden of being the one person to whom the church looks for significant guidance in the life and work of the church. The vast majority of churches—approximately two-thirds in the Southern Baptist Convention—have only the pastor, with no other staff. There is no way the pastor can be absolutely excused from the responsibility of leading in church planning. But, similarly, there is no way for the whole responsibility to be placed rightly on the pastor. The pastor must be an influencer of the planning but not the lonely doer of it all.

The Church Council and the Pastor Lead in Planning Church Ministries

In most churches which have planned ministries, the Church Council is the group with whom the pastor works to lead in developing the plans. Research has indicated that in more than 95 percent of the churches of the Southern Baptist Convention which say they use a Church Council, the pastor chairs the Council. This Church Council brings together leaders of the major church program organizations—Sunday School, Church Training, music ministry, Woman's Missionary Union, Brotherhood, and the deacons. In some churches, key committee personnel, as well as some staff leaders, are related to the Council. Together these leaders, with the help of the pastor, study the needs. They propose major goals and plans for meeting them. Then they relate their individual program organizations to the planning process by leading their planning groups to do detailed planning to support the church's broad goals.

Planning Is Hard Work

This kind of planning involves a lot of work. The pastor, staff members, church program organization leaders, committee chairmen and members, and many others will spend great amounts of time if they are to have an effective church ministry plan. But remember, they will also likely see far more accomplished as a result of their planning than they would without it. And they will experience personal growth and development in the process.

There often is a feeling that a great part of the work is finished with the completion of the planning. That is an accurate notion. Although much work remains after planning is initially completed, a major part of the work of ministry is accomplished when good plans have been made under His will.

Major Types of Planning

Up to this point we have looked in rather sweeping fashion at what ministry planning is, why leaders develop church ministry plans, and who should lead in the planning. Let's turn now to a more detailed look at some of the features of the process.

Basic Operational Planning

First, consider two major types of planning that should occur in every church. One type is in the area of the basic operational life of the church. If you should keep track of all the things your church does for a period of time, you would find that most of the activity is in this area of basic operations. These are the things you do on a continuing basis. They are mostly essential things that are done regularly, if not routinely. They are things you do to survive at the base, the church itself. You conduct worship services. You have Sunday School, Church Training, and missions education. You sing. You visit the sick. You marry the people. You bury the dead. You comfort the bereaved. These and many other things you do in season and out of season because you are a church. In much of this basic operation, the mode is one of reacting to things which occur, over many of which you have little or no control. Is there planning to do in these basic operational areas? Indeed there is.

In basic operational planning, the general thrust is to make the ministries more effective in quality, more efficient in process, and less consuming of resources. The concern is to make the base, the church, the best that it can be. Many churches make the mistake of planning and working only on operational things. They "strengthen the stake" but they do not "lengthen the cord." The first is necessary, but is eventually self-defeating without another type of planning. That type we call "advance" or growth planning.

Planning for Advance

Planning for advance is at the growing edge of the church. In this planning, you reach for new people to be brought to Christ, new ministries to be developed, new needs to be met. Here you plan for extraordinary increases in numbers. You also plan for extraordinary improvement in quality, such as in training of workers. Here, too, you consider the validity of ministering to those with special needs, and those in unique circumstances. Even major strengthening of the base operations might be considered advance. It is important for the base of be strengthened. The lengthening cords must have strengthened stakes to which to be anchored.

In developing church ministry plans leaders should consider the needs both in terms of the basic operational areas and in areas for advance. They should lead the church to plan for ministries in both.

Focusing on Annual Planning and Long-Range Planning

Another way of viewing and doing church ministry planning is to focus on annual planning and on long-range planning. Most of the detailed planning of a church's ministries would likely fall in the area of annual planning. This involves the pastor, the Church Council, the organizational councils, and some church committees as they plan the annual cycle of ministry events, emphases, and continuing programs.

Annual planning needs to consider both operational and advance areas. Also, most of the annual planning probably should be done in relation to implementing church *tasks*. In Southern Baptist life, a task in this context is described as *a basic, continuing activity of primary importance to the life and work of a church.* One can find the listing of tasks in books such as *Educational Ministry of a Church* (Tidwell), *Christian Education Handbook* (Powers), and *A Church on Mission* (McDonough). They include such ministries as reaching persons for Bible study, witnessing to persons about Christ and leading persons into church membership, equipping church members for discipleship and personal ministry, equipping church leaders for service, providing musical experiences in congregational services, witnessing and ministering through music, engaging in missions activities, teaching missions, leading the church in the accomplishment of its mission, proclaiming the gospel to believers and unbelievers, caring for the church's members and other persons in the community, and interpreting and undergirding the work of the church and the denomination.

Three Basic Principles in Planning

There are more tasks than we have identified here, but these are representative of the total group. There are three basic principles to consider in annual planning related to tasks.

1. The Church Itself Is the Basic Unit

The first principle of good annual planning is that *the church itself is the basic unit.* Neither Sunday School, Church Training, music ministry, Woman's Missionary Union, Brotherhood, the deacons, the church staff, the church committees, nor any one individual is the basic unit to consider. The church is the basic unit. The implications of this principle are many. Among them is the fact that the interests of the church, the overall fellowship, must have priority over the interests of any other entity, in or out of a church. Those outside might include the association, the state convention, the Southern Baptist Convention, and others. The churches do not exist so that other entities or bodies will have a support base. The external entities exist to assist churches to fulfill their purpose.

Groups inside a church need to be ready to give way to the

interests of the total body on matters like calendar, personnel, and money. In cases of conflicting requests, most often the subgroup in a church, such as one of the church organizations or any of its components, should give way.

Those who lead in determining what the total church's plans require must make a practice of planning far enough in advance so that other entities in the church can gracefully make their plans without conflict. One example might clarify how this principle applies in a church. Suppose the Church Council schedules a revival series well in advance. The dates are set. The church approves the calendar. Sunday School classes, training groups, workers' planning meetings, and other important events should give priority to what the church has approved. They should find other ways and times to do the work they would have done at the time of the scheduled revival.

2. All Tasks Are Church Tasks

A second important principle in church ministry planning is: *all tasks are church tasks.* They are the responsibility of the total church, even though in many churches certain organizations in the church have primary responsibility for their implementation.

The implications of this principle are many. One implication is that a church which is not big enough in its membership to warrant having all the recommended organizations still has the responsibility of finding ways to accomplish its tasks. And there are ways to work on these tasks without all of the recommended organizations. This is not a heresy! It is simply saying that a church which does not have a functioning Church Training organization still has the responsibility to accomplish the task of equipping church members for discipleship and personal ministry. A church which does not have a Woman's Missionary Union or a Brotherhood organization still has the responsibility for the tasks of teaching missions and of supporting missions. These and all the other tasks are *church* tasks.

Another implication is that in a church which does have the organizations recommended for implementing its tasks, the tasks are not the "property" of the organizations. They are still church tasks and must be duly subject to the will and the processes of the church. This means, among other things, that church organizations play by the rules of the church in planning, scheduling, enlisting and training leaders, funding, and in policies and procedures related to other actions. All tasks are church tasks.

3. Tasks Must Be Planned in Relationship

A third principle is: *tasks must be planned in relationship.* They must not be planned as though there were no other tasks of the church. Planners can find many ways for tasks of various organizations to be planned in complementary fashion, so as to strengthen and help one another. For example, while it is considered a pastoral ministries task to lead in proclaiming the gospel to believers and unbelievers, the Sunday School can plan to complement pastoral ministries in this task by the ways the Sunday School does its work of reaching persons for Bible study, witnessing to persons about Christ, and leading persons into church membership.

Other organizations can find ways to work together as they plan to implement their tasks. This is an arena which can be a model of God's children working together, graciously considering one another, and supporting one another, thereby strengthening the total church and its ministries. This way the church can have a *church* ministry plan, not just an accumulation of plans of many groups without unity.

Long-Range Planning Usually Extends for Several Years

The other type of planning we mentioned is long-range planning. This kind of planning considers what a church should plan to do to meet the studied needs in and out of its fellowship over a seven-to-ten year period. It usually is done by a special committee of a church and requires careful leadership over many months to develop. Good long-range planning considers the same functional areas as do other types of planning: purpose, objectives, program, organization, human resources, physical resources, financial resources, and controls. The committee recommends church goals, strategies, and action plans which are projected over the years of the plan. Such planning can give annual planning a very fine context in which to operate. The church approves the long-range plan. Major items are processed again for church approval as they come up on the long-range timetable. Plans may be reviewed and revised along the way as needed.

Help Is Plentiful for Those Who Lead Planning

There are many materials available to help leaders in planning church ministries, both in annual planning and in long-range planning. There are usually revised planning guides for use by the Church Council and organizational councils. There is a long-range planning notebook for use by church committees for long-range planning. Each year the major leadership magazine for each of the church program organizations and for church leaders in administration carry simultaneous planning features, usually in the spring and early summer editions.

Several state conventions have planning materials tailored for use by churches in their state for annual planning. There are associational, state convention, and Southern Baptist Convention calendars, and other helps available. Church leaders are wise to consider these materials, and to incorporate them into their planning at all points where they can contribute.

Suggested Format for Annual Planning

The following brief format for developing your church ministry plans might be helpful, especially in annual planning:

1. Establish and/or review your church's statements of purpose and objectives.
2. Identify areas of need for planning, both in basic operations and in areas for advance.
3. Set worthy goals that are attainable but challenging, measureable, and time-phased.
4. Suggest major strategies, approaches to reach each goal. This is your plan of action.
5. Develop the details of your plans, drawing upon program organizations and committees.
6. Correlate the proposed plans into a calendar of activities for church approval.

7. Coordinate financial planning to assure funding for the ministries.
8. Include evaluation criteria and periodic reviews of progress as appropriate.
9. Give positive leadership to the implementation of the plans.
10. Repeat this cycle for next year's plans.

Church leaders in planning must learn to be patient with one another and with others. It probably took your church quite some time to get in the condition it is in. With patience, good planning, and His help, maybe it will not take quite so long to develop effective church ministry plans that will see the church approaching its potential in bringing persons to God through Jesus Christ.

Summary

The fellowship we call church should be on the move in ministry. It should have a clear understanding of purpose. It needs specific objectives. Purpose and objectives should come to reality in a ministry plan. This plan is the church program.

A good ministry plan can lead a church to make progress in unity. It can develop leaders and members. It can help bring others to Christ.

The pastor usually should be the leader in church planning. The Church Council should work with the pastor in annual planning. A special committee is usually the best way to do long-range planning. Both annual and long-range planning should take into account basic operational planning and planning for advance.

Most annual planning relates to implementing church tasks. It is essential to the best planning that key principles be observed.

There are numerous helps available for those who lead in planning. These materials are coordinated to make the work of church leaders more feasible.

Leaders should develop and use a format for planning that meets their needs. They must also learn to be patient.

Learning Activity Suggestions

1. Based upon your church's present organization, list the positions of those who would serve on the Church Council to be responsible for annual planning.

2. List ten needs in your church's present basic operational areas for which there should be specific annual planning. List five needs in your church for planning for advance.

3. Review the three suggested basic principles for planning to implement church tasks. For each of these principles write a brief illustration of how they might relate to ministry planning in your church.

Note

1. Gaines S. Dobbins as quoted by Elmer Leslie Gray, "The Road We've Traveled," *Church Administration* (January, 1965), p. 13.

5
Designing Church Organization

Now in these days when the disciples were increasing in number, the Hellenists murmured against the Hebrews because their widows were neglected in the daily distribution. And the twelve summoned the body of the disciples and said, "It is not right that we should give up preaching the word of God to serve tables. Therefore, brethren, pick out from among you seven men of good repute, full of the Spirit and of wisdom, whom we may appoint to this duty. But we will devote ourselves to prayer and to the ministry of the word." And what they said pleased the whole multitude, and they chose Stephen, a man full of faith and of the Holy Spirit, and Philip, and Prochorus, and Nicanor, and Timon, and Parmenas, and Nicolaus, a proselyte of Antioch. These they set before the apostles, and they prayed and laid hands upon them. And the word of God increased; and the number of the disciples multiplied greatly in Jerusalem, and a great many of the priests were obedient to the faith (Acts 6:1-7, RSV).

Ideas This Chapter Includes

Biblical examples of organization

Definition and benefits or organization

Determining the need for organization

Principles of good church organization

Sample possibilities of organization

Contents of a church constitution

Steps in starting a new church

A church is a very special and unique creation. It is a fellowship. It is an organism, a unit of life. It is not primarily an organization. But it does have needs for organization.

There are people who resist the idea of a church being organized. Some think of organization as something out of place in a church. Some even doubt the idea that organization can be biblical. People who believe this are poor students of God's Word.

Examples of Organization

The Bible is plentiful in its examples or organization. God Himself is a God of order, not of chaos. Just one illustration from each of the Testaments will serve to show that organization is not antibiblical.

Moses

Probably the most fruitful passage in all of literature on leadership and organization is found in Exodus 18:13-27. One who reads this passage should find many ideas which even modern writers and other specialists in management discuss.

This is the account of Moses receiving some significant management counsel from his father-in-law, Jethro. Someone, with a keen sense of humor, developed an organization chart showing the plight of Moses before and after Jethro helped him reorganize. (See Charts 1 and 2). In the traditional-looking box chart format Moses is shown as the person responsible in forty-nine boxes, plus the leader's box at the top of the chart. His responsibilities listed on the boxes range through the alphabet, from agriculture, banking, baptism, and bartering to transportation, travel, water, and welfare. In classes it is usually pointed out that there is nothing for the letter "Z" of Moses' chart. Some astute student usually mentions that Moses' wife was named Zipporah. But our conclusion is that a man who was as busy as Moses doesn't have time for his wife! This painful conclusion points up the sad plight of many who lead in churches without adequate help through good organization.

There follows some very sound instruction for Moses regarding his role, the roles of qualified persons who should be placed in positions of responsibility to help bear the load, and this important promise: "If you do this, and God so commands you, then you will be able to endure, and all this people also will go to their place in peace" (v. 23, RSV). Their needs would be met!

Moses did what Jethro advised. And he didn't let Jethro leave until he had installed the plan!

The Twelve Apostles

Instances of organization abound in the New Testament. The great scholar A. T. Robertson, in *A Harmony of the Gospels for Students of the Life of Christ,* showed an interesting fact about the twelve apostles. He presented the four lists of the apostles in vertical columns side by side. The lists come from Mark 3:16-19; Matthew 10:2-4; Luke :14-16; and Acts 1:13. In these lists one can readily observe that Simon Peter is always listed first. Some take that to mean that Peter was the head of the apostles. One can discount that, in light of the fact that Jesus was their Head!

It is true that Peter was always listed first. On closer observation, one can see that the next three after Peter are the same in each list, but not always in the same order: James, John, and Andrew; then Andrew, James, and John, and so on.

The fifth person in all the lists is Philip. The next three are the same, but again in varied order: Bartholomew, Matthew, and Thomas; then Bartholomew, Thomas, and Matthew; then Thomas, Bartholomew, and Matthew. Philip is the only one who is consistently in the same position.

So it is with the last four. James, the son of Alpheus, is in the number nine position, followed by Thaddeus, Simon, and Judas Iscariot, who was omitted from the list in Acts.

Here is what Robertson said about this, adding that the scholars Bengel, Broadus, and Clark agreed:

> Observe the three groups of four, headed by Simon Peter, Philip, and James the son of Alpheus, respectively. The great variety in the arrangement of the other names makes this uniformity significant. It seems clear that there are three recognized groups among the apostles.[1]

The agreement of even these great scholars doesn't necessarily make it true that the apostles were organized. But it

Chart 1

Disorganization

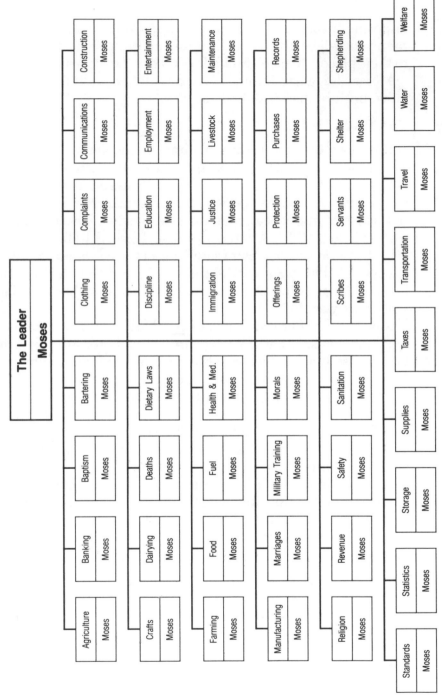

The Leader

Moses

| Agriculture | Banking | Baptism | Bartering | | Clothing | Complaints | Communications | Construction |
| Moses | Moses | Moses | Moses | | Moses | Moses | Moses | Moses |

| Crafts | Dairying | Deaths | Dietary Laws | | Discipline | Education | Employment | Entertainment |
| Moses | Moses | Moses | Moses | | Moses | Moses | Moses | Moses |

| Farming | Food | Fuel | Health & Med. | | Immigration | Justice | Livestock | Maintenance |
| Moses | Moses | Moses | Moses | | Moses | Moses | Moses | Moses |

| Manufacturing | Marriages | Military Training | Morals | | Offerings | Protection | Purchases | Records |
| Moses | Moses | Moses | Moses | | Moses | Moses | Moses | Moses |

| Religion | Revenue | Safety | Sanitation | | Scribes | Servants | Shelter | Shepherding |
| Moses | Moses | Moses | Moses | | Moses | Moses | Moses | Moses |

| Standards | Statistics | Storage | Supplies | Taxes | Transportation | Travel | Water | Welfare |
| Moses | Moses | Moses | Moses | Moses | Moses | Moses | Moses | Moses |

Chart 2

Organization

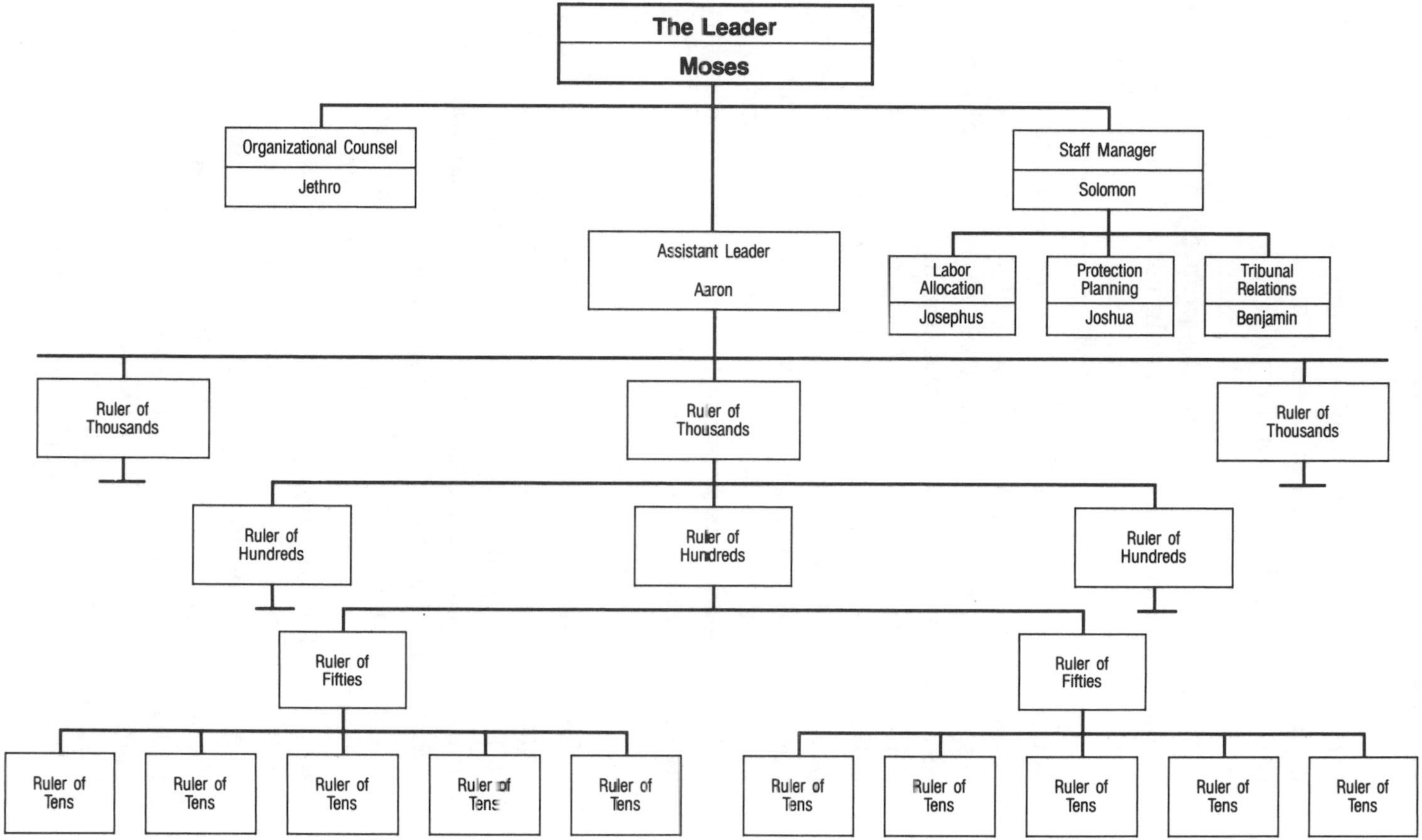

The Leader
Moses

Organizational Counsel
Jethro

Assistant Leader
Aaron

Staff Manager
Solomon

Labor Allocation
Josephus

Protection Planning
Joshua

Tribunal Relations
Benjamin

Ruler of Thousands

Ruler of Thousands

Ruler of Thousands

Ruler of Hundreds

Ruler of Hundreds

Ruler of Hundreds

Ruler of Fifties

Ruler of Fifties

Ruler of Tens

Ruler of Tens

Ruler of Tens

Ruler of Tens

Ruler of Tens

Ruler of Tens

Ruler of Tens

Ruler of Tens

Ruler of Tens

Ruler of Tens

certainly gives cause to think that they were. We have other indications that the apostles were interested in position since two of them had their mother speak to Jesus about their positions (Matt. 20:20 ff.).

The organization of the apostles probably did not come as a result of the work of a nominating committee! They might have been put in these groups by the Lord. Possibly they could have emerged quite naturally to their positions. The thing to notice here is that in the Bible there seems to have been organization. And it was this group to whom Jesus gave the responsibility to carry on His work. As a result, millions have received the gospel. That's good organization!

It really isn't *good* organization that people resist. It usually is either *poor* organization or *too many organizations*. Most people have had enough of organizations without clear purposes and objectives and programs. It is possible to have too many organizations calling for your participation and support. Churches need to study seriously their organization and try to avoid these indicators of poor organization.

Definition of Organization

Let us turn our attention to consider what might be *good* organization for a church. That is what we want to advocate.

There are many possible definitions or organization. This one is very simple and task oriented: *Organization is the arrangement of persons to get a job done.*

The common elements in organization, that is *good* organization, include some pattern of structure, some design—an *arrangement.* To bring life and meaning to this arrangement, one must bring *people.* As in team sports, one can mark the playing area and indicate where the players are to position themselves to begin the action. But the real organization appears when the players come onto the playing area and the game begins. They have a *job to do,* and they begin to do it. This is their purpose in being organized. Again, the elements are an arrangement, people, and a job to do.

Benefits of Good Organization

Good organization in a church offers some worthwhile benefits. Let us look at a few of these benefits of good organization.

First, *good organization distributes the work load.* As Jethro told Moses about his assignment, "The thing is too heavy for you; you are not able to perform it alone" (v. 18, RSV). That certainly is true of ministry and the work of a church. No one person is big enough or good enough to do it all alone. There must be others to share the work load, and there needs to be good distribution of the load.

Second, *good organization places responsibility where it belongs.* God has given a variety of gifts. Each recipient is responsible for the best use of his or her gifts in relation to the whole body, the church. With each person fulfilling his or her responsibility, the whole body can progress toward its goals.

Third, *good organization reduces confusion.* The work load is well distributed. The responsibility is placed where it belongs. Confusion is minimized.

Fourth, *good organization helps avoid unnecessary duplication of effort.* Duplication of effort is at best a waste, and at worst counterproductive. Some of the most glaring instances of poor organization at this point occur not in small churches but in large ones. For instance, in a very large church of several thousand members two secretaries were maintaining duplicate files of the master church member records, each apparently not knowing that the other was doing this. This had gone on for quite some time before the duplication was discovered. That was poor and costly duplication of effort. Good organization helps avoid this kind of happening.

Determining the Need for Organization

There are times when the best response to the impulse to add organizations is to test the need in the light of certain questions. It is possible that the need is not for more organizations. Ask questions like these:

Is there really a job to do? If the answer is affirmative, proceed with other questions. If not, stop the action to organize!

Does the need fall in the responsibility area of an existing officer, committee, or organization? There are numerous instances in churches in which positions, committees, or additional organizations were created unnecessarily because the responsibilities of existing officers, committees, or organizations were not clearly known. If the responsibility is already placed, deal with the need in terms of getting the job done with the existing organization. Don't add organization in such a case. If, for example, there is a committee which should be taking care of certain needs but is not, work to get that committee to function. Find what the problem is and work to overcome it. One creates more possible difficulties by failing to do so.

Can one person do the job effectively? If so, there are only a few exceptions which would call for you to have a group of persons organized to do a one-person job. For example, although one person could probably do an effective job of counting the church offerings, there are good reasons why the counting should be done by several persons. But in most instances, if the job can be done effectively and acceptably by one person, avoid creating a committee or other organization involving several persons.

Can a special group do the job as a temporary project? Perhaps an ad hoc committee would be more appropriate than a permanent or standing committee. For example, if your church celebrates the anniversaries of its founding in five-year or ten-year intervals, you might question whether you should have a permanent committee to plan church anniversary celebrations. And who would want a permanent pastor selection committee?

The whole point of these and other such questions is to plan to get the needs met effectively with as lean an organization design as possible. There is no virtue, and there might be some vice, in having more organizations than are needed. Try to avoid this problem.

Principles of Good Church Organization

There are certain marks of good church organization that distinguish it from poor organization. Some are even principles, axiomatic truths which are universally valid. Let us look briefly at some of these marks.

Good church organization will do these things:

1. Reflect the church's theology

2. Lead toward clearly defined goals

3. Be almost as simple as possible

4. Be flexible

5. Group similar jobs together

6. Match responsibility with authority

7. Establish clear guidelines

8. Keep congregational authority clear

Organization Reflects the Church's Theology

Let us look at each of these and try to clarify what we mean by them. Would you agree that good administration should grow out of good theology? That is what we mean when we say that a church's organization should reflect its theology. It should be compatible with what we say we believe, not only about God but also about the dignity and worth of individuals. Further, there should be no organization design for a congregationally governed church which violates the tenets of congregational democracy. For example, a church whose deacons, committees, councils, staff, pastor, or any other group or individual function as a final filter through which matters *must* be screened in order to get to the church body is in danger of not being a fully congregational body. There is a significant difference in having *required* approval by certain groups or individuals in a church and in having *optional consultation* from those same groups or individuals.

There is often wisdom in the counsel of many. But in a Baptist church this consultation needs to be distinguished from having to have approval. Any individual or group of a church, any committee whose parent is the church, should have right of access to the church body. A church should clarify in its procedures how this access is assured.

A church committee might wisely seek the counsel of deacons on matters of importance to the church; but to require a committee of the church to have its work approved by the deacons is questionable in light of Baptist theology.

It is possible to have our cake and eat it too! We can have the counsel of any others in a church without having to have their approval. Then let the church make its own decisions.

Organization Leads Toward Clearly Defined Goals

Good church organization should be goal oriented. It should not exist without purpose or direction. It should be designed to enable a church to accomplish its goals. If the goals are temporary, perhaps the organization should be temporary. If the goals are continuing, the organization for reaching the goals should be continuing.

In a study of one church's committee structure, the study group (a special, temporary committee) came upon a committee called the Planning Committee. They asked the chairman to recall the origin of this committee. Several years earlier it had begun as a Building Planning Committee, to lead in the addition of another needed building. The building was completed, but the committee continued to have things referred to it by the church. Over the years its name was shortened informally, not by church action. The chairman told of the most recent matter the church had referred to the committee: How should the church divide the revival love offering between the guest evangelist and the guest musician? The chairman happily accepted the recommendation that the Planning Committee be thanked and dissolved and that future decisions about the church's finances be considered by the church Stewardship Committee.

Organization Should Be Almost as Simple as Possible

Good church organization should be kept almost as simple as possible. The simplest possible organization is one which is run by one person. The possibilities in such an extremely simple organization range from dismal failure and ineffectiveness to a rigid dictatorship. Neither of these is right nor desirable.

As a healthy body should be just big enough for maximum effectiveness, so should an organization. Too little organization allows for poor distribution of the work load. Too few are probably called upon to do too much, and many miss the blessings of meaningful work in the church. Too much or too many organizations tend to be cumbersome and ineffective.

Church size and program plans, along with other factors, should help you to find the right organization design for your church. Churches have come to have organization along a wide variety of lines. Historically, Baptist churches have organized their total membership in several ways. In addition to pastors and deacons, Baptist churches have had officer positions of the whole congregation. There are the moderator, trustees, clerk, and treasurer. The moderator is often the pastor, though not in every case. The person in this position presides over meetings of the church members for transacting business for the church. The trustees serve as representatives of the congregation and under the congregation's instructions to do such things as are necessary in the signing of legal and business documents and other similar matters. The clerk maintains church membership records and handles essential correspondence and recording related to the membership and to its decisions in session. The treasurer is the official financial officer of the church and operates, as do the others, under the instructions of the church.[2]

Another way churches organize for ministry is known among Baptists as the Deacon Family Ministry Plan. Since nearly half the church members are not members of the largest educational organization, the Sunday School, churches need some organized way to relate to the needs of every household. In the Deacon Family Ministry Plan, each household is assigned to a deacon for regular contact and ministry. Without such a plan, most congregations have no ministry to those who do not attend the education ministry organizations or the church services or worship. The Deacon Family Ministry Plan has produced significant improvement in the ministry of a church to its members.[3]

Chart 3

Possibilities for Church Organization

Type of Unit Position	Suggested Units or Positions				
	Churches with Fewer than 150 Members*	Churches with 150 to 399 Members	Churches with 400 to 699 Members	Churches with 700 to 1,499 Members	Churches with 1,500 or more Members
Staff	Pastor Music Director[1]	Pastor Music Director[1] Secretary[2] Custodian[2] Pianist/Organist[1]	Pastor Minister of Music and Education Secretary Custodian Organist[1] Pianist[1]	Pastor Minister of Music Minister of Education Secretaries[3] Custodians[3] Organist[1] Pianist[1] Age-Division Ministers[3]	Pastor Associate Pastor Minister of Education Minister of Music Business Administrator Minister of Recreation Evangelism/Outreach Minister Age-division Ministers Organist-Music Assistant Family Life Minister Secretaries[3] Custodians[3] Hostess Food service personnel[3]
Deacons	Deacons (1 deacon per 15 family units; minimum of 2 deacons)	Deacons (1 deacon per 15 family units)	Deacons (1 deacon per 15 family units)	Deacons (1 deacon per 15 family units)	Deacons (1 deacon per 15 family units)
Church Officers	Moderator (Pastor) Trustees Clerk Treasurer	Moderator Trustees Clerk Treasurer	Moderator Trustees Clerk Treasurer	Moderator Trustees Clerk Treasurer	Moderator Trustees Clerk Treasurer
Church Committees	Nominating Stewardship Missions Evangelism	Nominating Property and Space Stewardship Ushers Missions Preschool[4] Evangelism	Nominating Property and Space Stewardship Personnel Missions Preschool History Ushers Weekday Education[4] Public Relations Evangelism	Nominating Property and Space Stewardship Personnel Missions Preschool Food Service History Ushers Weekday Education[4] Public Relations Evangelism	Nominating Property and Space Stewardship Personnel Missions Preschool Food Service History Ushers Weekday Education[4] Public Relations Evangelism Other committees as needed
Service Programs	Media Services Director	Media Services Director (up to 3 workers) Recreation Director	Media Staff Recreation Staff	Media Staff Recreation Staff	Media Staff Recreation Staff

Special Ministries		Senior Adult Ministry	Senior Adult Ministry Singles Ministry	Senior Adult Ministry Singles Ministry	Senior Adult Ministry Singles Ministry	Senior Adult Ministry Singles Ministry Intergenerational Activities
Coordination	Church Council	Church Council WMU Council S. S. Council Brotherhood Council	Church Council S. S. Council C. T. Council Music Council WMU Council Brotherhood Council Division Coordination Conferences	Church Council S. S. Council C. T. Council Music Council WMU Council Brotherhood Council Division Coordination Conferences	Church Council S. S. Council C. T. Council Music Council WMU Council Brotherhood Council Division Coordination Conferences	Church Council S. S. Council C. T. Council Music Council WMU Council Brotherhood Council Media Services Council Division Coordination Conferences
Bible Teaching	General officers and organization for each age division	Departments for each age division	Multiple departments as needed	Multiple departments as needed	Multiple departments as needed	Multiple departments as needed
Church Training	Church Training Director Age-group leaders[4]	Member training groups and departments for each age division Equipping Centers New Church Member Training	Member training groups and departments for each age division Equipping Centers New Church Member Training	Member training groups and departments for each age division Equipping Centers New Church Member Training	Member training groups and departments for each age division Equipping Centers New Church Member Training	Member training groups and departments for each age division Equipping Centers New Church Member Training
WMU	WMU Director Age level organizations as needed	Age level organizations as needed	Age level organizations as needed	Age level organizations as needed	Age level organizations as needed	Age level organizations as needed
Brotherhood	Brotherhood Director	Baptist Men Royal Ambassador groups as needed	Baptist Men Royal Ambassador groups as needed	Baptist Men Royal Ambassador groups as needed	Baptist Men Royal Ambassador groups as needed	Baptist Men Royal Ambassador groups as needed
Music Ministry	Music Director[5] Pianist Choir	Music Director[5] Organist Church Choir or Ensemble Age-division choirs when possible	Age-division choirs Instrumental groups as needed	Fully developed Music Ministry	Fully developed Music Ministry	Fully developed Music Ministry

[1] Volunteer or part-time
[2] Part-time
[3] As needed
[4] If needed
[5] Person serves as program leader and staff member

* NOTE: It is important to encourage, in any way possible, churches of 150 members or less to have choir, recreation, and other needed ministries even though directors or other leaders for that activity might not be listed in column one of this chart.

There are other ways churches are organized to accomplish their purpose. If you would like more specific suggestions, look at Chart 3. There you will see suggested church organization for five sizes of churches. There are suggestions for staff, deacons, church officers, church committees, service programs, special ministries, coordination, Bible teaching, church training, mission organizations, and music ministry for each size church.[4]

Organization Should Be Flexible

Good church organization should be flexible. It should expand as the needs justify expansion. In the instance of organization in which growth is desired, such as in Bible teaching classes or departments like the Sunday School, new units should be formed as worker-member ratios and additional known prospects for enrollment suggest. New units grow faster than older, established units. And they reach more people for Christ. These are verifiable facts in the history and in the present experience of Sunday Schools that are growing. Planned expansion or addition of organizational units is a key factor in growing a church. There are known worker-member ratios, maximum membership sizes, and other factors which church leaders should consider in expanding or adding organizations.

In some instances the organizational flexibility concept calls for reducing or contracting the organization. Circumstances change, and sometimes the need or organizational units diminishes. One can use the same good ratios and other factors that were used to expand or to add to the organization to determine when organization should flex downward. Again, in a Sunday School situation, there are years when the number of persons in a given group in an age-graded organization might be considerably smaller than in other years. In other years the flexibility concept would say, "Reduce the number of units to fit the need." Obviously, most of us enjoy enlarging and expanding instead of reducing the organizations, because more organization should be associated with reaching and ministering to more people. We are right when we are concerned about reaching and ministering to more people.

Organization Groups Similar Jobs Together

Good organization groups similar jobs together. The flower committee doesn't usually plan the church budget! There are many tasks in a church. Those tasks which are similar should be grouped together and assigned to persons with gifts and other qualifications for performing particular tasks. If needs continue to arise which do not seem to fit any of the present organizational responsibilities, that might suggest the need for some reorganization or for some additional organization. First, see if the newly discovered need can be met adequately and appropriately by existing organization. If not, then make the needed changes. In any case, try to put related or similar tasks together for assignment.

Organization Matches Responsibility with Authority

Good church organization matches responsibility with authority. Some people don't like the use of the word *authority*. They prefer to call it "freedom to act." Whatever one calls it, a person in a place of responsibility in an organization needs to be authorized or free to do what is right and necessary to get the assignment done. Of course, there should be known limits to that authority or freedom. But authority or freedom must be exercised within those limits.

Seward Hiltner wrote,

> If even God felt it wise and right and essential to risk his purposes and his love through fallible human instruments, who is a minister to be unwilling to acknowledge that his ministry must be risked through fallible human beings who are, in actual fact, no more fallible than he?[5]

Organization Establishes Clear Guidelines

Good church organization establishes clear guidelines. It sees that groups and individuals are informed regarding duties, responsibilities, and limits. For example, if there is a staff member or a committee who has responsibility for money expenditures, the procedures and limits of spending are better made known *before* rather than *after* the fact of some violation. Good organization works toward preventing as well as solving problems.

Organization Keeps Congregational Authority Clear

Good church organization keeps congregational authority clear. Certain decisions should be reserved for the church body to make. Matters like calling ministers, changing the name or location of the church, altering the constitution or bylaws, and qualifications for membership who will serve in church positions are some of the decisions no individual or group should make for the church. Obviously there are many other items a church should decide for itself.

Constitution and Bylaws

The work of the church calls for the organism to be organized. Staff, deacons, educational and other ministries, committees, even the entire church membership needs to be organized appropriately and effectively. It is recommended that a church carefully and prayerfully take the time to develop a church constitution and bylaws to reflect the consensus of its members about how a church is organized. The pamphlet called "The Church Constitution and Bylaws Committee" could help further in the preparation of a constitution and bylaws.

Constitution

Every Baptist church has fundamental truths or principles held by its members and others to be important in determining how the church will relate to its members and to others. When these fundamental principles are embodied in a written document, they are called a constitution. In the absence of a written document, a constitution may be implied in a church's established beliefs, organizations, practices, and customs. In reality, every church has a constitution, either written or implied.

A constitution reflects the basic truths and the settled rules of action related to the function, the direction, and the control of the church. In a written constitution are placed those items most treasured and enduring, such as these:

1. A preamble, which sets forth the purpose of the constitution

2. The church name, in the official form to be used for church business and legal purposes

3. A statement of the church's purposes or objectives

4. A statement of basic beliefs of a doctrinal nature

5. A church covenant reflecting the commitment of members to one another in light of their commitment to God

6. A statement of polity and relationships

Bylaws

Bylaws are written rules or guidelines agreed upon by the church members for regulating and directing the church's own internal affairs, dealing with others, and government of the members. Bylaws focus on the procedural matters which might be subject to change more often than would the constitution. These are the kinds of items frequently found in church bylaws:

1. A church membership section, with instructions regarding how members are received and oriented, rights of members, membership termination, and discipline of members;

2. A section on church officers and committees, naming them and at least characterizing their responsibilities, and indicating their selection and termination processes;

3. A church program organizations section, with information about the purposes, officers, organization, tasks, and church relationship of each organization;

4. A section on church program services, identifying and relating their tasks to church programs and leaders;

5. A Church Council section, explaining the group's work in relation to church ministries and programs;

6. A section on church ordinances, setting forth the modes and procedures for their observance;

7. A church meetings section, establishing the patterns of meeting for worship, special services, regular and special business meetings, establishing a quorum, and identifying the rules of order the church will observe as authoritative;

8. A section on church finances, establishing procedures

and responsibility for effectively caring for the church's financial resources;

9. A church operations manual section, particularly useful in large churches, authorizing and directing the establishment and maintenance of church policies and procedures in the many areas of administrative concern in a church;

10. A section on amendments, indicating how both the constitution and the bylaws may be changed in an orderly manner.

A Special Committee Prepares the Constitution and Bylaws for Church Approval

Preparing a church constitution and bylaws is a significant experience for a church. These documents should represent in a positive way the church's intent and design for orderly ministry. They should reflect both for the members and for others an accurate image of the church in all areas included in the documents.

The church should elect a special (temporary) committee to prepare and present for church consideration a written constitution and bylaws. Once the church has voiced approval for creating this special committee, the church nominating committee should prayerfully nominate committee members, giving careful consideration to assure adequate representation of the major segments of membership. If possible, the number of committee members should be between five and nine persons. A group in this range can work smoothly and efficiently while also being representative of the church membership. It might be useful to include at least one member who is familiar with the church's past constitutional stance and experience. The membership of the committee should be chosen from devoted, knowledgeable, mature church members, including qualified persons from several age divisions—youth, young adult, median adult, and senior adult. The nominating committee should consider the leadership experience in church life and draw on this experience in selecting nominees to serve on this special committee.

The church should instruct the special committee regarding its purpose and duties and its tenure. The purpose of the committee is to prepare and present for church consideration a written constitution and bylaws. The duties might be stated as follows:

1. Decide what items (articles, sections, etc.) the constitution and bylaws should include.

2. Compile the statements written by committee members for all items to be considered for inclusions in the constitution and bylaws.

3. Present the proposed constitution and bylaws to the church for consideration.

4. Recommend that the church adopt the constitution and bylaws, after due consideration and modification.

5. Determine a plan for further distribution and bylaws. These suggestions might be included in the bylaws.[6] (See Appendix A for a sample constitution and bylaws.)

Churches Should Be Incorporated

Churches are well advised also to take the necessary steps to become legally incorporated. By this act of declaring itself to be incorporated, and completing the necessary legal instrument or instruments to accomplish this, a church is declaring to all who might be concerned that it is to be treated collectively as a body of persons, rather than singly as individual members. Incorporation is simply declaring legally for society what Baptists believe to be our theological position. The church is a body of persons, not individuals who are free to sign contracts, transact business, commit the church for debts, or other such acts as individuals. Also, individuals in the incorporated church are not subject to legal process as are individuals apart from the body, the church. Without incorporation, in some states, each individual is singly responsible for the total indebtedness of the church. That is not practical nor right.

A church can avoid many complications by being incorporated. This is a fairly simple step, but calls for the assistance of a competent attorney. The registration of the incorporated status usually is with the office of the secretary of state in whatever state the church is located. There are forms to which attorneys have access for completing this process.

Organizing New Churches

It is important for existing churches to be aggressive in properly beginning new churches. How to begin and organize a new church is a vital concern. Consider these nine basic steps.

1. Select a Church Missions Committee

A planning group, such as a church missions committee, is essential in starting a new church. This group must be competent, carefully chosen, well trained, and totally committed to Christ and to starting churches.

2. Select the Area of Need

The Church Missions Committee should identify the area where the new church is needed. This can be decided by contacting the associational missions office, making studies, and gathering data about the selected place.

3. Prepare the Church

The church should be prepared to become a "parent" church. The pastor should preach motivation sermons that present the need for a new church. Church groups should visit the prospective area and discuss ways they can help. Workers should be trained to serve in the new church. The parent church should vote to sponsor the new project.

4. Cultivate the New Church Field

The selected area for the new church should be surveyed to identify the unchurched and unenlisted people. Systematic, get-acquainted visitation should follow the survey. Ask interested Christians to pray for the new church project. Choir concerts, children's recreation programs, Big A Clubs, lay-witness teams, and many other activities can be used in community cultivation.

5. Begin Mission Fellowships

Friends made through cultivation activities may be gathered in home Bible fellowship groups. Informal worship services may be conducted. Some may become new Christians; inactive Christians may be revived. These groups may form a nucleus of believers to make up the new congregation.

6. Organize the Mission Chapel

The Bible fellowship groups will begin to grow into a visible congregation. The relationship of this new congregation, or mission chapel, to the parent church should be determined. A program of activities should be designed. As the congregation grows, the program can be expanded.

7. Arrange Mission Chapel Finances

The handling of finances for the new mission chapel should be worked out by the church missions committee. A budget should be formulated and adopted by the parent church.

8. Provide the Facilities

The use of temporary facilities is strongly encouraged until the new congregation develops to the point that it can share in decision making. Delaying the burden of paying for property is recommended if the situation permits. Energy costs and interest rates should be considered. Constructing simple, attractive buildings that can be used for both Sunday School and worship services is encouraged.

9. Constitute the New Church

Constituting the mission congregation into an autonomous church should be delayed until there is maturity of leadership, stability in doctrine, basic core support, and ability in self-government. The church missions committee should consider prayerfully all of these things before recommending that the mission become a church. Detailed guidelines on constituting a church are available.

Good church starting requires careful planning, hard work, and much prayer. The Holy Spirit is basic, and He will enable you to be an effective church starter.

These nine steps are basic and essential to a good experience in church starting. They are discussed in detail in *Guide for Starting New Churches,* which may be obtained from any Baptist state missions office. Two films also are available from the Baptist missions office: *Planned Parenthood for Churches* and *A Church Is Born.*[7]

Good organization does not guarantee success. But poor organization can almost assure failure. The Father has given some the gifts for organization. Why not see what He would do through His church at work in an orderly fashion?

Summary

A church is an organism with needs for organization. The Bible is plentiful in examples of organization. Illustrations from Moses' experience and from the apostles' design are instructive.

People resist poor organization or too many organizations. Good organization is the arrangement of persons to get a job done. Specific benefits accrue from good organization.

It is helpful to get answers to certain probing questions before rushing to add organization. Often these are overlooked, resulting in poor organization.

Key principles of good organization can help a church greatly. The recommended organization for a church is that which is just adequate for effectiveness and efficiency. Sample designs for churches of different sizes are suggested.

It is recommended that a church develop its own constitution and bylaws, and that it become incorporated. It is also important that churches begin other churches. Nine steps in starting new churches, as suggested by the Home Mission Board of the Southern Baptist Convention, are offered. The church deserves our best efforts in organization as well as in every other dimension of our concern.

Learning Activity Suggestions

1. Write your own single-sentence definition of organization. Identify the major elements in your definition. What are the implications of your definition for your church?

2. From Chart 3 write a comparison of your present church's organization with that of the similar size on the chart. What changes would you suggest for your church organization?

3. Write a brief illustration from the context of your church

for each of the eight suggested marks or principles of good church organization.

4. Examine the sample constitution and bylaws in Appendix A. What do you see as its strengths? Its weaknesses? What changes would you suggest for your church if this were its constitution and bylaws?

Notes

1. A. T. Robertson, *A Harmony of the Gospels for Students of the Life of Christ* (New York: Harper and Bros., 1950), pp. 271-272.

2. For further help regarding the work of these church officers see sources like the pamphlet, "Church Officers: Moderator, Treasurer, Trustees, Clerk," articles in the magazine, *Church Administration,* and *Church Officer and Committee Guidebook,* by James A. Sheffield. All of these are published by the Sunday School Board of the Southern Baptist Convention, 127 Ninth Avenue, North, Nashville, Tennessee 37234.

3. For help regarding the Deacon Family Ministry Plan see the materials listed in the current "Church Materials Catalog," free annually from the Baptist Sunday School Board.

4. Bruce P. Powers, editor/compiler, *Christian Education Handbook* (Nashville: Broadman Press, 1981), pp. 130-131.

5. Seward Hiltner, *Ferment in the Ministry* (New York: Abingon Press, 1969), p. 85.

6. Charles A. Tidwell, "The Church Constitution and Bylaws Committee" (Nashville: The Sunday School Board of the Southern Baptist Convention, 1977), pp. 3-5.

7. These steps are from the free pamphlet, "Nine Steps in Starting New Churches" (Atlanta: Home Mission Board, SBC, 1983).

6
Administering Human Resources

Do unto others as you would have them do unto you." There, in one sentence, is the greatest subject there is, by the greatest author that ever lived. There is the main principle of good management in its simplest form.—Lawrence A. Appley[1]

Ideas This Chapter Includes

Specialness of people

Distinction between volunteers and staff

Aspects of working with volunteers

Approaches to staff administration

Administering the total membership

A church is people. They are people who have voluntarily received Christ as Lord and Savior. They have chosen to band together to try obediently to live the way of Christ and to share with Him in bringing people to the Father.

Specialness of People

It is crucial when we look at the topic of this chapter that we be reminded of the specialness of these people, the church. It is vitally important that we see people not just as resources. People are more than means to ends. Leaders in a church, of all people, must regard and treat one another and others with the dignity and sense of worth that people deserve. This deserving may or may not come from what individuals have themselves earned. More important, it comes from the esteem in which God Himself holds persons.

God Formed People with Special Creative Care

God made people in His own image. Genesis 2:7 indicates that it was with special creative care that the Lord God *formed* man of dust from the ground and breathed into his nostrils the breath of life, and man became a living being. This high point of God's creative acts was so special that the writer used a uniquely chosen word for this forming of man, different from the language used to describe his creative acts in the marvelous account of Genesis 1. Persons are the centerpiece of His creation. In the simple words of the oft-used expression, "God didn't make no junk." People are special! Church leaders must regard and treat them so.

It could be more important to a church leader to spend whatever time is needed to let His Spirit convince of the dignity and worth of people than to rely first on any knowledge, skill, or technique of administering a church's human resources which anyone might suggest. People in and out of churches are starving in our time for the milk of human kindness to nourish their spirits. It is almost unthinkable that people who claim Christ as Lord would intentionally deal with one another or with others in ways that are personally or institutionally selfish or insensitive.

People Must Not Be Treated as Things

As we consider administering a church's human resources, it is imperative to remember that we are considering people and not things. Although at times the needs call for firm, even disciplinary actions, church leaders must try always to be fair, kind, redemptive, and Christlike as they work with people.

Human Resources Administration Is Complex

Human resources means people. But we need to look more closely at the term. It means leaders. It also means those who follow. It involves the commitment and availability of people. It includes their knowledge and skills, and their capabilities, their potential. It extends to all their assets, whether personal, financial, or some other category. Human resources is a tremendously complex and vital area for administration in a church.

Volunteers and Staff

Human resources come in a variety of categories. One way of viewing them for administrative purposes is to see them in two clusters: volunteers and staff.

Volunteers

By volunteers we usually mean those whom we make no attempt to compensate financially. In Baptist life the volunteers are rarely those who come forward without some individual recruitment to offer their services as might be needed. Actually, they are more often draftees! They are selected and recruited to serve without financial remuneration in positions like that of Sunday School teacher, deacon, choir member, Church Training leader, missions organization leader, committee member, and any of a large number of such positions. Most are church-elected.

Staff

Financial compensation.—When we say staff, we usually mean those who serve in places of responsibility at the request of the church or one of its organizations and who receive some financial compensation for these services rendered. This is not to suggest that they work mainly nor only for the financial remuneration. Most often, like the volunteers, they chose to respond to the needs and the invitation to serve.

Called of God to minister.—The church expects certain staff members to evidence a call of God to minister. Pastors, ministers of education, ministers of music, age-group ministers, and many other ministering positions illustrate those of whom churches expect a divine call. It is the opinion of this writer that those of whom the church expects a divine call to minister should, in every instance, also be presented to the church for a call by the church. Those who serve in church staff positions other than that of a God-called minister could be employed by a church personnel committee in consultation with the minister who would supervise their work. Office, clerical, and manual workers illustrate this latter group. It is often a plus that those who work in office, clerical, or manual positions feel a distinct sense of mission in their work. One should not discourage that. But unless the church requires of them a divine call in order to qualify for a position, they can and should be dealt with in somewhat different ways than those who must be God-called in order to qualify for the position. A call by church vote is one of the differences.

Equipping.—All are called to be disciples. All disciples are called to minister in the general sense of the term. Some are given to be "apostles, some prophets, some evangelists, some pastors and teachers, to equip the saints for the work of ministry, for building up the body of Christ" (Eph. 4:11-12, RSV). All of these are a church's human resources.

Major Aspects of Working with Volunteers

Let us consider now the area of working with volunteers in a church. How do you administer this great sector of human resources in a church? What is the scope of the assignment? Many books address the answers to these and other questions about working with volunteers. We can only highlight key areas here as we overview the field.

These are some of the major parts of the job of working with volunteers:

1. "Pray . . . the Lord . . . to send out laborers."
2. Develop qualifications for leaders.
3. Identify needs for leaders.
4. Discover potential leaders.
5. Provide basic preservice training for potential leaders.
6. Recruit for specific positions.
7. Give specialized training for specific positions.
8. Continue development through on-the-job training and continuing education.
9. Supervise leaders.
10. Motivate them.
11. Evaluate their work.
12. Recognize them appropriately.

One could probably add other items to this list. Look at the list again. Think of possible ways or techniques that relate to these suggestions. Which of these might have some application to those who serve as church staff workers?

Pastor's Support of Volunteers Is Vital

Administering the work of volunteers in a church involves several possible individual and group approaches. For example, it is important for the pastor as an individual to support by word and deed the work of the volunteers. As appropriate, the pastor should publicly demonstrate support for those who serve. People who had some part in the lives of those who make commitments at invitation time in the worship services could be suitably recognized and thanked. The pastor could emphasize the joys of service as well as the needs for persons to serve from time to time. The pastor's presence and counsel in meetings of workers as well as at the stated times of work are important indicators of interest and support. It is wise for the pastor to find ways to encourage and support the volunteers.

Pray for Laborers

Let us look now at each of these suggestions about what is involved in working with volunteers. The Lord gave the right instructions about where to begin to get workers. In Matthew 9:36-38 He looked with compassion at the crowds who

> were harassed and helpless, like sheep without a shepherd. Then he said to his disciples, "The harvest is plentiful, but the laborers are few; pray therefore the Lord of the harvest to send out laborers into his harvest."

A church should be in prayer continuously for the Lord to lead them in discovering those who should serve in the work of the church. It is the firm conviction of many veteran church leaders that in any church there are the potential workers for what the Lord wants to do in that church. He is the kind of Lord who does not expect of us what we cannot do with His help. But He is also the kind of Lord who *does* expect us to do what we *can* do with His help. We need His help to find and enlist and develop workers. We must ask Him to lead us to those who should serve, and to lead them to respond to His leadership. Individuals, groups, and the church as a whole should pray for the workers needed.

Some of the groups which need to relate to administering the work of volunteers are the church nominating committee, the Church Council, the organizational councils—like Sunday School, Church Training, music ministry, Woman's Missionary Union, and Brotherhood councils—and church staff members such as the pastor, the minister of education, and age-group ministers. Working together, these groups and individuals should develop qualifications for leaders. The church nominating committee, which has general responsibility for overseeing the worker recruitment for all church organizations, might develop general qualifications to be met by persons who serve in any church organization. Then a given group, like the Sunday School council, might use a worker's covenant to guide its workers in developing qualities that are important to the work of Sunday School.

Identify Positions Which Need Leaders

Leaders of various organized ministries should work together to identify the positions which need leaders. The various organizational councils, for instance, should be responsible for this in their organization. The church nominating committee might need to assist those which do not have a leadership council as they determine the needs.

Discover Potential Leaders

Discovering potential leaders should be the concern of everyone in a church. But, lest this important step be neglected because "everybody's business is nobody's business," a church needs to have definite strategies for discovering potential leaders. A talent or interest inventory of all church members, along with a record of past service, is one good way to help discover potential. The systematic survey of new church members as they come into the church is another. Still another good way is to call periodically upon leaders of adult groups in the church to recommend confidentially members of their groups who might be ready for some preservice training with a view to the possibility of going to work. Church staff members and other leaders should be constantly alert to those who might serve in some way and should make it a matter of prayer and frequent conversation among themselves.

Provide Preservice Training for Potential Leaders

Leaders of church organizations, with the help of church staff personnel, should provide basic, preservice training for potential leaders. There are materials available to help in this regard. Plan and schedule the training. Recruit potential workers individually for this special basic training. At the end of the training, the trainee might be ready for recruitment for a specific place of service. Churches need to have such training in progress throughout the year if they expect to meet the needs for qualified, trained workers.

Recruit Workers for Specific Positions with the Help of the Nominating Committee

In most churches a church nominating committee coordinates and oversees the recruitment of workers for church organizations. Some very large churches might need to have a committee on committees to share the load with the church nominating committee, enabling the nominating committee to concentrate on the program organizations and their needs —the Sunday School, church training, music ministry, Woman's Missionary Union, and Brotherhood. The committee on committees might staff all church committees and possibly assist in the deacon selection.

If more than one group is involved in enlisting workers, there is added need for coordination of their efforts, lest there be more confusion than progress. It is critically important in a church that the worker enlistment take place in an orderly manner. The church nominating committee must be given the authority to approve or to disapprove a prospective worker *prior* to the enlistment contact if you wish to do well in staffing the organizations.

Persons whose units need workers should help in the search for prospective workers. Upon discovering such a prospect, the leader should contact the church nominating committee with a request for permission to enlist. If granted, the person who would supervise the new worker should conduct the enlistment interviews and report back to the committee. Then the committee presents the nominee to church for election.

Some feel they can't take time for such a procedure. A church can ill afford *not* to take the time to do it right. More time is lost by poor, disorderly procedures than by using good ones. By following good procedures church leaders can take into account the gifts of the individual, the overall needs of the church organizations, and the priorities within the church's ministries.

Some churches have assigned the recruitment of volunteers to church staff personnel or have allowed staff personnel to do most or all of it. In my opinion, this is unwise. Staff persons might render valuable assistance in the enlistment, but the one who is to work most closely with the enlisted worker should present the challenge, the requirements, the resources, and all the facets of the job to the recruit. This supervisor will have a vital part in all the rest of the aspects of the new worker's experience as a worker.

Give Specialized Training for Specific Positions and Continue Development

The supervisor will help in the arrangements for specialized training and other continuing development in on-the-job training and continuing education opportunities. The Church Study Course should be of major assistance in this regard. It is a comprehensive, simple plan for developing workers for almost any church assignment.[2]

Motivate Volunteer Workers

The supervisor who enlisted the new worker should oversee the work in such a way as to enable the worker to succeed in the assignment and to realize the joy of success in personal fulfillment. The supervisor leads in motivating the workers— unleashing those inner springs in the workers which cause them to want to do what they need to do.

Evaluate Their Work and Recognize Workers Appropriately

The supervisor evaluates the work in both formal and informal ways. The supervisor compensates the workers with suitable and deserved recognition, praise, and in other ways. Others might also share in these actions with the supervisor. In fact, the entire church might have a variety of ways of motivating, evaluating, and compensating workers. These are very important actions, not only with volunteers, but also with church staff personnel.

Staff Leaders Should Develop Volunteer Workers

Church staff leaders should concentrate their energies on developing the volunteers. As these volunteers multiply and develop, the whole work of a church is advanced. Those who are in places of service, like a Sunday School teacher, grow and develop more than those whom they serve. Church staff people have the opportunity to lead in an advanced level education and ministry endeavor as they help the volunteer workers do the work—growing and developing as they serve.

Administering the Church Staff

Administering the staff of a church is, for many churches, a major part of administering human resources. There is some truth in the notion that, in the long term, a church can rise no higher than its leaders. The principal service a staff can render a church is to provide leadership in the church's ministries. This is especially true of the ministers a church might have. These, in turn, are heavily dependent upon those who render the support services of a church, such as the office, clerical, and manual workers who might be employed as staff.

*A Special Committee to Assist
in Securing Ministers*

Churches approach their staffing needs in a variety of ways. Almost all churches have as their first need that of securing a pastor. This they usually do with the help of an ad hoc committee. The name for this committee in current Southern Baptist literature is the pastor selection committee, though most churches probably still use the term *pulpit committee.* This committee develops job qualifications, gets information on possible candidates, selects the one they feel led of God to present to the church in view of a call by the church, and assists in the settling of this new pastor into the new "field." Then this committee's work is terminated. Some churches use a similar approach in securing ministers other than the pastor.

Personnel Committee

A church personnel committee gives essential help in staff administration on a year-round basis. This committee usually works with the pastor, who is considered the chief of staff, in all matters pertaining to church staff administration. Church staff members might have occasions when they would be assisted or consulted by this committee.

The personnel committee assists by such services as surveying the needs for new staff positions or for staff position adjustment. The committee is a church committee and is accountable to the church. As long as the pastor is responsible as the chief of the staff, the committee works closely with the pastor. They develop job qualifications and job descriptions. They might help by preparing organization charts. They recommend for church approval the staff policies and procedures, which, along with other information, might be developed in the form of a personnel manual. They could assist in establishing work schedules, especially for those whose work is on a specified hours basis, such as a forty-hour workweek or other hourly workers. All of this needs to be done in consultation with supervising staff personnel. The committee can assist ad hoc committees in the search for ministers for the church. They could assist supervising staff ministers in employing office, clerical, and manual workers.

The personnel committee should develop the church's compensation plans, including the salary plan and the benefits for all paid personnel. Within the percentage of the church budget or the dollar amount allocated in the budget planning processes of a church, the personnel committee, not the stewardship or finance or budget planning committee or the deacons, should recommend staff salaries and benefits for church approval. These compensation plans should be presented to the church in as full detail as the church desires, and should be endorsed by church vote. The benefits should include such items of need as housing, transportation expenses, hospital/medical protection, retirement planning, vacations, holidays, medical leave, employee development, conventions and conferences, continuing education, and other such needs as might arise in a given situation, such as time allowed for service opportunities.

In several parts of this committee's work, there is need to consult with other committees and individuals or, at times, with the entire church membership. For instance, this committee should give major help in preparing the church for the arrival of a new person on staff. This should include such things as ample publicity, appropriate reception activities, and assistance in getting settled into home and job. The minister staffers especially need thorough introductions to the church members. And all staffers might need this committee's help in orientation and getting established in their positions.

Other Areas of Concern Regarding Volunteers and Staff

Thus far we have focused on the leaders, both the volunteers and the staff members. There is much more that could be said in regard to these. Good communications and appropriate supervision need to be developed. (See Appendix B for articles on these subjects.) There is a need for regular and appropriately frequent meetings, such as staff meetings and planning meetings.[3] Interpersonal relationships and caring fellowship are vital areas.[4] Integrity, trust, and love are areas of essential concern. But we must conclude with a word about the total church.

Administering the Total Membership

What shall we say about administering the human resources represented by the total membership? They are at once the objects of a church's ministries and the resources of these same ministries. Let us begin by saying that the administering of the many organizations, committees, and other groups, such as deacons, as implied up to this point, will help take care of the administering of the church membership. But beyond that, those who lead, either as volunteers or as church staff members, must begin proper administration with *esteem* for the members. There is no room for such adversary notions as "I" or "we" *versus* "they" or "them." Such notions usually stem from some presumed sense of superiority and should not have place in a Christian body.

Further, church members deserve the kind of care that shares in their joys and in their sorrow. They need and deserve leadership. They are entitled to fair consideration and to equality of opportunity, privilege, expectation, and responsibility in keeping with their readiness. They should be led to participate by voice and by vote as needed. They have responsibilities to give financially and to receive support through prayer and personal encouragement. They should give and get cooperation. They should be fairly represented as occasions warrant. They should receive reports and information as the body may desire and without inferences of suspicion as to motive when not deserved. They have the right to determine their leaders, to hold them accountable, and to recall them by church-endorsed processes.

Baptist churches observe majority rule. They are democracies or "Christocracies." Christ is the Head of a Baptist church. In determining the mind of Christ, the members of a local body trust that a majority can discern the mind of Christ on a matter more likely than can a minority. Usually that is accurate in its results. It is more apt to be accurate more often in churches in which the human resources are administered in the manner and by procedures intended in this chapter.

Summary

Church leaders, of all people, should recognize the specialness of people and relate to them accordingly. This insight is probably more important than any amount of knowledge, skill, or technique of administration.

Human resources is a complex area of administration. It includes administering volunteers, church staff, and the total membership. It includes leaders and members. It relates to their knowledge, skills, capabilities, potential, assets, commitment, and availability.

Staff ministers are expected to manifest a call of God to minister. They are given to equip the members in ministering.

There are numerous aspects of working with volunteers. The pastor's support of volunteers is vital. The church nominating committee and others work with the pastor and the staff to mobilize the volunteers. Church staff leaders should give priority in their ministry to developing volunteers.

Special committees and the church personnel committee assist in administering the church staff. These committees work with other committees of a church and with the pastor and staff to bring about the desired effectiveness and efficiency of the staff.

The total membership requires administration. Much of this is accomplished by the appropriate operation of the church's organizations as presented in a previous chapter.

Learning Activity Suggestions

1. Based on a study of Scripture, write a five-hundred-word statement of the specialness of mankind and its implications for administering a church.

2. Compatible with the concepts in this chapter, write a nominating committee procedure that begins with the needs for workers already identified and concludes with church election of the workers recruited. Limit the procedures to a single page.

3. Secure a copy of the current catalog for the Church Study Course. Prepare a five-minute speech for delivery to a meeting of all Sunday School workers in a church, informing and encouraging them about the possibilities the Church Study Course offers them in training for their positions in the Sunday School.

4. Secure a copy of the pamphlet, "The Church Personnel Committee." Extract in writing the major items in the work of this committee and put them in a list on a single page.

5. Identify the major problem you feel exists regarding administering the total membership. How should one deal with this to bring about an approach to solution?

Notes

1. Lawrence A. Appley, *The Management Evolution* (United States of America, American Management Association, Inc., 1963), pp. 14-15.

2. Information about the Church Study Course is available in an annual, free catalog by that name from the Baptist Sunday School Board, 127 Ninth Avenue, North, Nashville, Tennessee 37234. It describes a multifaceted approach to training church leaders and members that offers more than one hundred diploma plans (each diploma requiring the study of six books), with more than five hundred courses in dozens of study areas. Free computerized records services assist church leaders in conducting this comprehensive training plan.

3. There are several excellent resources that give help in considerable detail regarding staff meetings and planning meetings. In addition to church program organizational manuals, such as Sunday School Administration books and leadership periodicals for these organizations, consider these books in particular (from Convention Press unless otherwise noted):

Jerry Brown, *Church Staff Teams that Win*
Bruce Grubbs, *Helping a Small Church Grow*
Leonard E. Wedel, *Church Staff Administration* (Broadman Press)

4. These additional Convention Press books could help:

Bob Dale, *Growing a Loving Church*
Reginald M. McDonough, *Growing Ministers, Growing Churches*
Ernest E. Mosley, *Priorities in Ministry*

7
Administering Physical Resources

He is the image of the invisible God, the first-born of all creation; for in him all things were created, in heaven and on earth, visible and invisible, whether thrones or dominions or principalities or authorities—all things were created through him and for him (Col. 1:15-17, RSV).

Ideas This Chapter Includes

Priority of people over things

Major categories of physical resources

Guidance in curriculum materials selection

Services of the Church Architecture Department

Approaches to funding buildings

Need to balance expenditures and not neglect
other vital areas

Good church administration begins with the purpose of a church. Then come church objectives, church ministry plans, organization, and the administration of human resources. Physical resources follow next.

Priority of People

For some, the mention of church administration means immediately the administration of physical resources. Usually one thinks of the buildings of a church. The physical resources, the buildings and other things of a church, are important. But they are not first, either in priority or in time.

There were churches in history long before there were

church buildings. In fact, it was not until about the third Christian century that churches had buildings of their own. They met in homes, borrowed buildings, open areas, caves, and other places. They did not have curriculum materials, books, pianos, hymnals, record forms, parking places, office equipment, air conditioning, or any of the many physical items with which we presently are concerned.

As time progressed, churches began to feel the need for buildings of their own in which to gather for their various reasons—worship, instruction, and fellowship. Through the centuries, churches have come to have quite large holdings of physical things that can be useful in fulfilling their purpose. It is about the administration of these physical things that this chapter is concerned.

Physical resources are the *things* of church administration. Things come after people in their importance. In our concern for the proper administration of things, we must always take care to put people before things. Given the choice of people or things, the choice should be people. But it is true that our ministries to the needs of people can often be enriched and made more effective if we have the things we need. Further, we are concerned that these things be right things, in the right quantities, in the right condition, at the right place, at the right time, and at the right price. There is a stewardship concerning the physical resources with which administration is rightly concerned. When this stewardship is realized, then the things physical can best serve their purposes in a church.

Categories of Physical Resources

In this chapter we shall consider four major groupings which call for administrative attention. They are: (1) Curriculum materials; (2) Supplies; (3) Properties; (4) Equipment and furnishings.
We will identify and describe each of these categories and the particular kinds of administrative responsibilities each requires.

Curriculum Materials

First let us consider curriculum materials. These are the materials of various kinds and forms which a church uses to help in educational and growth experiences. Almost all program organizations in churches of our time use some curriculum materials.

Periodical literature and undated materials are major curriculum aids.—One commonly used type of curriculum material is periodical literature. The most common of these periodicals is the quarterly. In Sunday Schools, for example, both pupils and teachers have periodicals, quarterlies, to assist in their understanding of the Bible. The very youngest children, the preschool groups, usually do not have quarterly magazines, but may have other periodical literature, such as leaflets for a single Sunday's emphasis. And there are periodicals that are monthly pieces rather than quarterlies.

Sunday School, Church Training, Woman's Missionary Union, Brotherhood, and music ministry, as well as pastoral ministries individuals and groups like the pastor and deacons, have periodical literature to guide them in their learning and in their service. These materials are available primarily through the Baptist Sunday School Board, the Woman's Missionary Union, and the Brotherhood by way of their national offices or through Baptist Book Stores. Periodical literature comprises the largest single category of curriculum materials used in most Baptist churches. Most of the periodical literature is designed for one-time use on specific dates, but there is a growing body of what is called "undated literature" which is also gaining widespread use. Denominations other than Baptist have their own sources for curriculum materials.

Books and other materials are important curriculum items. —Books such as those with Convention Press, Broadman Press, or the Sunday School Board imprint are another important part of the curriculum materials category. Major uses of these are the teacher and leader training in a church and the general Christian growth of church members. The Church Study Course system for leader and member development has more than five hundred courses, most of which use one or more books. (See the note in chapter 6 about the Church Study Course.)

Various other learning aids and some supply items might be classified as curriculum materials. Films, filmstrips, audiocassettes, recordings, videocassettes, and other items illustrate these.

A church needs to have administrative procedures to assure that they have what they want and need in the category of curriculum materials. The church itself is responsible for its curriculum—the experiences provided for its members and for others in the name of the church. And the church itself is responsible for the curriculum *materials* used in its ministries. The church has the right and the responsibility to guide and to control these materials.

A church must guide and control its curriculum materials selection and use.—There needs to be a known procedure for selecting and approving curriculum materials. One good way is to have the Church Council recommend to the church the line or lines of curriculum materials to be used. Any exceptions to the use of approved lines should be considered and approved by the Church Council or the church itself. Such a procedure will help assure that the church is aware and approves of what is offered in the name of the church. Other areas of administrative concern regarding curriculum materials might include processes for ordering, securing, distributing, using, storing, and financing the materials. The denominational publishers are happy to provide suggestions regarding all of these areas. Consider using a curriculum selection checklist, such as that in Chart 4[1] of this text, to help assure the wisest selection of curriculum materials. Responsible groups like the Sunday School Council and the Church Council should use an instrument like this to guide them as they make choices about curriculum materials.

Church Supply Items

A second category of physical resources in a church is that of church supplies. These are primarily the expendable items a church might use, such as record forms, art supplies for use in educational and other programs, paper, chalk, erasers, pencils, and numerous other similar items. These might seem to be somewhat insignificant in relation to the larger concerns of a church. But they become even more significant by their absence when you need them. How many times have you been in meetings at the church when the progress of the meeting had to wait while someone searched for paper, pencils, chalk, or an eraser?

A simple plan, with responsibility clearly assigned, would take care of most needs in a church regarding supplies. One person conceivably could oversee the inventory of supplies and be responsible for purchasing new ones as they are needed. In some instances there need to be plans for distributing, using, and storing, as well as paying for these items. In some churches there need to be separate but coordinated plans regarding teaching supplies, office supplies, maintenance supplies, and kitchen supplies.

Considerable financial savings can result from planned buying both of curriculum materials and of supplies of various kinds. A church needs to develop its own plans for purchasing these and other items.[2]

Good stewardship requires planning for church supplies. —It is important in good stewardship of resources that there be planned ways for ordering, securing, distributing, using, storing, and paying for church supplies. Many of the church supply items can best be secured locally or in a nearby city. It is good to have an established procedure for their purchase. There should be a continuous inventory of supplies, in order to help assure the timely restocking of items. Suitable quantity purchases can be very economical. Some items call for administrative suggestions for distribution, care, and use. Church staff members can work with volunteer leaders to determine how best to administer supplies in your church.

Church Properties

The third category is a very big one in many churches. This is the category of properties: buildings, grounds, and parking. The administration of these areas is quite demanding. Sometimes the responsibilities can be so time-and energy-consuming that they threaten a minister's effectiveness in other areas

Chart 4

Curriculum Selection Checklist

Use this checklist to compare lines of curriculum you might consider for use with a given age group. Secure samples of each line you wish to consider. Examine the materials carefully. Check each item on the list below. Indicate by _✓_ which line is best on each factor. Compare the basic pieces of each line: the pupil's material; the teacher's material. Choose and use the curriculum that best meets your needs.

| Factor to Consider | Curriculum Lines | | |
	A	B	C
1. There is ample, appropriate use of the Bible.			
2. The teachings are doctrinally sound.			
3. Doctrinal emphases are balanced.			
4. Coverage of the Bible is comprehensive.			
5. The educational philosophy is valid.			
6. Concepts presented are suited to the age group.			
7. Content addresses life needs appropriately.			
8. Teachings encourage appropriate responses.			
9. Methodology is properly related to content.			
10. Methods are suited to our workers' skills.			
11. Training materials are available to develop worker's skills.			
12. Learning activities are right for the age group.			
13. The materials support the church program.			
14. Materials advance purposes of this organization.			
15. Quality teaching/learning aids are readily available.			
16. Supplementary commentaries are available.			
17. Art use is in good taste.			
18. The layout is attractive to the user.			
19. The binding is sufficiently durable.			
20. The paper quality is adequate.			
21. The print size is right.			
22. The print is clear and easy to read.			
23. Uses of color in materials is attractive.			
24. Service for ordering, receiving, paying is good.			
25. Consultation in use of materials is available.			
26. Volume (number of pages) in each piece is adequate.			
27. The cost in relation to the benefits is suitable.			
28. The cost per comparable items is least.			
29. _____			

(Other factor we consider important)

| 30. _____ | | | |

(Other factor we consider important)

Based upon this comparison, curriculum line _____ seems best for us. It is available at the following address:

_____

_____

_____

of ministry. Once buildings, grounds, and parking are planned, constructed, and in use, there remain the concerns that they be paid for, properly used, and maintained.

Churches have many kinds of buildings.—There often is wide variety in the buildings of a single congregation. Many important decisions are made in the planning stages prior to construction of buildings that later affect their administration. There are auditoriums of several possible kinds. There is educational space for the various programs designed for different age groups. There might be recreation and other special activities space. There are kitchens and sometimes snack bars. There is space designed primarily for Sunday use. There might also be space designed for everyday use through the week. Some space must be used for combination purposes. No one person can adequately care for all the possible details related to many church buildings. And when you add to buildings the needs for grounds and parking, there is a huge set of responsibilities!

The Church Architecture Department offers help to Southern Baptists.—Southern Baptists are fortunate in having the consultative services of the Church Architecture Department to assist them in properly planning for their buildings, grounds, and parking needs. This department is housed at the Baptist Sunday School Board in Nashville, Tennessee. Their consultative services are free to cooperating churches of the Convention. In special instances of need for consultation related to landscaping and interior design, there is a charge made to the using churches to recover the cost of these special services. The same cost recovery service charge applies to special acoustical design consultation.

Without cost to a church, the department offers guidance in conducting building programs, selecting an architect, selecting a site, analyzing programs and planning space, designing quality and attractive buildings, selecting equipment and furnishings, financing a building program, and other areas. The department offers free consultation in its offices when committees and architects find it possible to come there. A consultant might visit for an on-site conference with a single church. There are free floor plan layouts and property development plans this department will design for a church's property and program needs. Consultants will review and critique architects' drawings.

Further free services of this department include reviewing and approving plans for Home Mission Board building loan requests. The department will supply upon request certain general information related to a church's building program planning, remodeling, and maintenance. Those in this department can recommend the manufacturers of building products, equipment, and furnishings. Free, too, are their special studies of the building exterior, the equipment and furnishings selection, and the layouts of kitchen, offices, and media library facilities.

The Church Architecture Department periodically offers special meetings in Baptist state convention areas, in associations, and for architects who might serve Baptist church congregations.

Equipment and Furnishings

The last cetegory we are considering in physical resources is equipment and furnishings. Some might wonder if these are included in properties. There is a sense in which they are definitely part of the church property. But there are good reasons to look at them separately. Office equipment, auditorium furnishings, recreation equipment, certain plumbing items, heating and cooling equipment, lighting equipment, tables, chairs, lecterns, sound equipment, audiovisual equipment, pianos, kitchen and food service equipment—these and other items are treated in contracts as different from the buildings. For example, casualty insurance which covers a church's buildings usually would not cover the equipment or furnishings unless they are specified as covered. Cost estimates for the construction of buildings do not include furnishings, although furnishings account for another 15 to 20 percent of the cost of adding usable space.

Equipment and furnishings are similar to buildings in their needs for administration. Someone must plan for and secure them. Some of them are to be constructed with the building. There needs to be guidance in the use of equipment and furnishings. They must be paid for, and they require some maintenance.

Policies regarding use of physical resources.—Properties and equipment and furnishings call for some policies regarding their use. Questions like these must be dealt with:

1. Who may use them?
2. Where and under what conditions may they be used?
3. What, if any, charge is to be made for their use?
4. Through what procedure does one need to go to schedule and use them?
5. Who is to be responsible for their care and their return to their previous condition?

Routine actions.—Preventive maintenance, repairs, housekeeping, and other routine actions must be planned and carried out. These actions help assure that the properties and the equipment and furnishings are available for the uses for which they were provided. Those who administer the church's physical resources must try to see that these resources are cared for and properly used.

Property and space committee.—A church property and space committee should be selected to assist and to advise in the administration of the properties and the equipment and furnishings, once they are acquired. If a church has staff members who supervise the care and use of these items, the committee should work in an advisory capacity to assist those staffers in getting the work done. The specific areas of this committee's assignment possibilities are printed in the committee pamphlet, "Church Property and Space Committee," and in other places. This pamphlet is available through the Church Services and Materials Department of the Baptist Sunday School Board.

There are other administrative responsibilities regarding physical resources. Physical security, such as protection from theft and fire, is important. Financial protection through appropriate insurance is needed. Legal protection through church incorporation should be provided. Use planning, organizing, systematizing, and other administrative skills and knowledge to make physical resources most efficient in the church's ministries of growing and helping people.

Church Building Program

A Valuable Resource

One of the most valuable items the Church Architecture Department makes available is a book, the *Church Property/ Building Guidebook* (Revised Edition with Energy Section), compiled by T. Lee Anderton, published by Convention Press. A summary of the contents of this detailed guide will serve to point out the multitude of concerns a church might consider about property and buildings.

Part I

The Three Essential Phases of a Building Program
> Recognizing needs—church action—appointing the committee—securing Church Architecture Department help—guidance materials
> *The Survey Phase*
> Determining surveys needed—community survey—property survey—building survey—checking structural condition of existing buildings—recommendations to church
> *The Planning Phase*
> Property use development—property acquisition—program graphics—tentative cost proposals—cost estimates on furnishings—the architect's schematics—reviewing the architect's schematics—Church Architecture Department reviewing schematics—reviewing cost proposals—considering alternatives—recommendations to church—project design—review of project design
> *The Construction Phase*
> Construction drawings—construction bids—furnishings bids—construction and furnishings loan—project construction—inspection of work—furnishing the building —final inspection—beyond construction phase: maintenance—financing

II. Structuring the Organization
> Types of organizational structure—determining the size committee needed—committee name—the large com-

mittee structure—organizing the steering committee—
qualifications of committee members—committee
chairman, vice-chairman and secretary's job descriptions—organizing subcommittees and work groups—the
simplified committee structure—minimum organization
structure—selection of committee members—training
the committee

III. Subcommittees and Their Functions

Organizing the Subcommittees

Publicity — church growth — property program —furnishings — finance — plans — construction — members
needed — duties of officers — purpose of each subcommittee — subcommittee relationships — work of
each subcommittee

Part II

IV. Studying the Church Community

Relating environmental conditions to church planning
—when to make a community study—who should make
the study—determining data needed—sources of information—population statistics—economic conditions—
social, educational, and cultural conditions—moral conditions—religious conditions—physical characteristics—
visual presentation of information—bar charts—line
charts—community map—values of community survey
—survey information forms

V. Space Needs for Church Programs

Relating program and space needs of worship—interim
and final auditorium—vestibule—pulpit platform—
choir area—choir rehearsal room—instruments—
auditorium seating—chapel—prayer room. Relating
program and space needs of Sunday School—Church
Training—Woman's Missionary Union—Brotherhood—
kindergarten, weekday schools, day care—offices—library—fellowship, dining, kitchens—recreation center

VI. Providing for Physically Handicapped and Exceptional Persons

Site planning for the disabled—parking, walks, and
ramps, entrance doors—planning the building for the
disabled—wheelchair and occupant dimensions—dimensions of individual on crutches—corridors, stairs, toi-
let rooms, department rooms, and classrooms

VII. Selecting, Retaining, and Working with an Architect
When to employ an architect—selecting an architect—
fee agreements—service of an architect—ownership of
documents—the owner's responsibilities—relationships
VIII. Planning Church Grounds and Parking Lots
Developing the master plan—a pattern for growth—
influences of codes and ordinances—zoning processes—
parking required—rules of thumb for land, building, and
parking space—utilizing property effectively—a realistic look at needs and possibilities—locating buildings by
use—relating buildings and grounds—circulation—re-
specting the site and neighborhood—the automobile,
safety, and convenience—improving function and appearance—landscaping—lighting—graphics—tying   it
all together—checklists
IX. Effective Use of Space
List of programs requiring space—using permanent
worship space—using temporary worship space—using
permanent educational space—using activities buildings
—using outside space for fellowship and recreation
X. Improving New and Old Through Good Design
Design means function and appearance—evaluating
your existing building—planning the new building—
professional assistance—making the buildings functional
—master plan—relation to other buildings and site—
program and organization—space and arrangement—
flexibility and change—access and corridor circulation—
safety—comfort and convenience—maintenance—making the building attractive—using art principles—providing unity and theme—exterior design—auditorium
exterior—educational building exterior—overall building complex—windows, doors, entrances—interior design—auditorium   space—educational   space,   corridors—other spaces—style, tradition, and design
XI. Designing for Low Maintenance
Recognizing   structural   deterioration—repairs—low
maintenance construction—selection of materials—preventive maintenance—inspections and scheduling—
care of grounds
XII. Financing for Building, Upgrading, and Maintenance
Financing a new building—consider total building budget—how to grow a building fund—how to conduct a

building fund campaign—where to get help for the campaign—types of loans—sources for borrowing money—issuing bonds—how to ask for and get loans—financing maintenance of existing space

XIII. Promoting the Building Program

Opportunities for promotion—promotional pointers—mediafor promotion—special program suggestions, site dedication, ground breaking, cornerstone laying—dedication day programs, new sanctuary, educational building, organ, memorials—continuing promotion

Part III: Rules of Thumb

XIV. The Energy Issue

The energy picture in the United States—energy crises and the church—implications of decreased mobility—moral and stewardship implications—church building implications

XV. Energy Conservation in Existing Buildings

Starting an energy management project—the energy audit—evaluation and implementation—building use survey—energy saving checklist—summary

XVI. Designing Energy Efficient New Buildings

Plan minimum space for maximum use—design for minimum heat loss or gain—design efficient lighting; design efficient mechanical systems—summary

XVII. Solar Energy

Passive solar systems—direct gain approach—indirect gain approach—the greenhouse approach—active solar systems—air solar systems—liquid solar systems—combination solar systems—summary

Glossary
Bibliography

Church leaders who follow the suggestions in this book will be well on the way toward good administration with regard to their building, grounds, and parking needs.

Financing the Building Program

Because of the tremendously heavy financial involvement many churches have in their properties, we should consider the major patterns by which churches deal with these financial concerns. Other financial administration concerns will follow in the next chapter.

It is important to establish that almost without exception it is the people of a church who pay for their own buildings and other properties. Very few churches have had their buildings given to them, and some of these have mixed feelings about the gift! Most often, the money comes from a broad base of the church members. The thing to be determined, then, is by what pattern or patterns the members will pay for their properties.

1. Conventional loans
2. Sale of bonds
3. Intensified giving
4. Planned accumulation of funds
5. Deferred giving
6. Other ways, including combinations of those listed above

The book *Church Property/Building Guidebook* has descriptions and suggestions about most of these ways of getting money to pay for buildings. The chapter titled "Financing Capital Improvements" written by this author in *Creative Church Administration* could also help. Let us identify and describe these funding approaches.

Conventional loans involve money borrowed from a conventional lending source. The majority of the money borrowed in a conventional manner from ordinary lending sources is borrowed from commercial banks, savings and loan (building and loan) associations, mutual savings banks, or insurance companies. The term *conventional* in this case has nothing to do with a denomination, a "convention." There are funds available for loan to churches from certain denominational agencies, but they usually are restricted for use in instances like new churches or in special needs in which a church has unique circumstances which prohibit borrowing from conventional lenders like banks. The Home Mission Board of the Southern Baptist Convention, through its Church Loan Division, is one of these denominational sources. Some Baptist state conventions also have organizations through which limited amounts might be borrowed. Most ordinary church loan needs would not qualify for loans from a denomination's limited funds.

The sale of bonds is another way of borrowing money for church building needs. A church usually needs professional help to use this method properly. A bond is a piece of paper the church gives to a member or friend who lends the church the amount of money specified on the bond. The bond is the church's promise to pay and includes the terms of repayment. The Securities and Exchange Commission has regulations regarding bonds that must be met by churches issuing them.

Loans of a conventional type and those acquired by the sale of bonds almost always involve paying interest. Borrowers are sometimes surprised to learn the amount of interest required for loans. It is common to pay back several times the amount borrowed because of the time and the interest involved in paying back loans. Borrowers should know how much interest might be involved as they consider this method of financing buildings.

To illustrate the cost of interest on borrowed funds, there is a general "rule of thumb" called the "rule of 72." Divide the number 72 by the annual percentage rate on a loan, and the answer is the number of years in which the borrowers will have paid back *twice* the amount borrowed. If you borrowed $100,000 at an annual percentage rate of 12 percent, divide 72 by 12. Borrowers then can see that in six years they will have paid back $200,000. This kind of information can help in the decisions about how to finance buildings.

Intensified giving by the members and friends of the church is another way churches use. This method is sometimes called the "cash pledge" method. Through a concentrated information, inspiration, and promotion effort, church members and friends are asked to make a commitment to give sacrificially above their regular gifts for a specified period of time, usually three years. This money is used to pay for the buildings. Not all churches can raise all the money needed in this manner. Some can and do. In this way they avoid long-term debt with its high interst. Usually there is some short-term debt, at least during the period of construction. But the payback period can be substantially shortened, and considerable money saved.

The Southern Baptist Convention through the Stewardship Commission and some Baptist state convention offices offers consultative services on a fee basis to assist churches in the intensified giving approach. Independent firms also offer such services, at significantly higher fees, to the churches.

Planned accumulation of funds is a common way for churches to get at least a start on financing buildings. It is good to begin such accumulation at the completion of one building period, looking toward the next building. The budget, special offerings on holidays and other special occasions, along with deferred giving plans, are ways to accumulate building funds for the future needs.

Deferred giving is still another way of producing funds for capital needs. Making the church the beneficiary of life insurance policies is one method by which some make a deferred gift. Others give securities, annuities, living memorials, bequests under wills, and other devices which benefit the church, and often, the individual who gives. The Southern Baptist Foundation and Baptist state convention foundations are among those from whom counsel about deferred giving is available.

There are other ways of funding buildings. Usually these other ways are variations of the ways already described. Often they are combinations of two or more ways. A church might find suitable ways to combine conventional loans with intensified giving and, in some instances, with bonds also.

It is important that as a church adds to its physical resources the church does not default on its responsibilities in other areas—such as missions support, compensation of the pastor and staff, and in ministries of the church. Such a balancing act calls for sincere, honest, and intelligent leadership by those who administer a church. Such leadership will include maximizing the use of present physical resources before spending more money for additional buildings. In some instances this involves scheduling the buildings for multiple shifts of use, as in Sunday School and worship services. Unused space, and that which has very limited time use, costs at least as much as that which is much used. In terms of human need, churches can ill afford not to make maximum use of what they already have before committing money to build more space.

Summary

Physical resources can make a significant contribution to the ministries of a church. But they are not the first priority of a church. People should come before things.

Curriculum materials, supplies, properties, and equipment and furnishings are the major categories of physical resources. A church must guide and control carefully its curriculum materials selection and use. Good stewardship requires planning also for supply items.

Church properties include buildings, grounds, and parking. The Church Architecture Department offers significant help to Southern Baptists regarding buildings, grounds, and parking. A major aid is the *Church Property/Building Guidebook*. The consultative services are also excellent.

Equipment and furnishings comprise a category of physical resources. These items are treated separately in many contractual matters, such as insurance.

Churches are heavily involved financially in properties. Church members pay for their buildings and properties in a variety of ways. When interest payments are involved, churches should learn and weigh the amount of interest before borrowing. Many churches find intensified giving to be useful. There are variations and combinations of methods. Some caution seems in order that churches not neglect other vital areas because of their physical resources.

A church needs policies to guide in the use of many of their physical resources. Also, preventive maintenance, repairs, housekeeping, and other routine actions are all important. A church property and space committee can give valuable assistance in administering the physical facilities. Security, financial, and legal protection are other areas of concern.

Learning Activity Suggestions

1. Using the curriculum selection checklist, secure two or more pupil's Sunday School quarterlies for the same age group and make a thorough comparison. Let one be a Southern Bap-

tist quarterly. Do the same for a set of teacher's materials for a specific age group.

2. Survey five or more churches in your area regarding their building debt. Ask such questions as these:

What is your total indebtedness for buildings and properties?

What is your total annual income for the past year? Figure the ratio of debt to income.

What is the annual percentage rate on the debt?

What is the amount of the annual payment on this indebtedness? What part of this is for interest? For principal? What percentage of your church's monthly income does your building payment represent?

What percentage of your church's monthly income goes for staff compensation? For missions?

How do you feel about your church's debt picture?

Notes

1. Charles A. Tidwell, "Administering Educational Support Services," *Christian Education Handbook,* Bruce Powers, editor/compiler (Nashville: Broadman Press, 1981), p. 205.

2. For more detailed help regarding administering curriculum materials and church supplies, see these books:

Marvin Myers, author/comp., *Managing the Business Affairs of the Church* (Nashville: Convention Press, 1981)

Christian Education Handbook Bruce P. Powers, ed./comp. (Nashville: Broadman Press, 1981)

Robert A. Young, *The Development of a Church Manual of Administrative Policies* (Louisville: Bel-Air Studios Church Directory Publishers, n.d.).

8
Administering Financial Resources

The earth is the Lord's and the fulness thereof,
the world and those who dwell therein;
for he has founded it upon the seas,
and established it upon the rivers (Ps. 24:1-2, RSV).

Moreover it is required of stewards that they be found trustworthy (1 Cor. 4:2, RSV).

Ideas This Chapter Includes

The important place of financial resources
in administration

Definition of financial resources

Ten major responsibilities in financial
administration in a church

The mention of administration in the context of the church soon prompts the typical person to think of finances. Administering the financial resources of a church is a tremendously important part of effective leadership for ministry. Good leadership regarding the church's financial resources is indispensable as part of the support system that enables a church to fulfill its purpose. Poor leadership in this area will almost certainly guarantee problems that hinder a church's effectiveness.

In other chapters we have seen the sequence of administrative areas we are considering in this text. Let us look again to see where financial resources fit into this scheme.

Importance

Leaders must lead a church to clarify its purpose. They must determine a church's objectives. They must develop ministry plans and design organization to implement the plans. They must administer resources—human, physical, and financial. And they must provide effective controls.

It seems clear from this sequence that administering financial resources is not the first concern of church administration. But don't be misled by its position in the sequence. Each of these areas of administration is like a link in a chain. If each link is strong, the chain is strong. If one link is weak, the whole chain is affected. Financial resources are required in order to provide physical resources to those persons who staff the organization, so that the ministry plans can be carried out. In this way a church can move toward its objectives and realize its purpose.

In this chapter we shall introduce the major administrative responsibilities regarding church financial resources. For each of these responsibilities we shall also suggest some ways of fulfilling the responsibilities. In reality, a given church will have to work out its own ways that seem to meet the needs best in its situation.

Definition

Many wise administrators use the term *financial resources,* and not just *finances* or *money.* That is not accidental. It is intentional. Even though most of this presentation deals with money, or finances, it is important to establish the fact that financial resources means more than money or finances.

Financial resources are the money, the knowledge, the skills, the attitudes, the commitment, which help make available those human and physical resources needed to implement the ministries of a church. Fortunately, church leaders don't have to put an exact monetary value on knowledge, skills, attitudes, and commitment. But they are indeed of value to a church. If a church had to pay an exact amount for them, the figure would be substantial! Many services are rendered in the life of a church that do not require payment in money. Members donate their services without keeping an account of the money value. We can be thankful for that!

Administrative Responsibilities Regarding Money

Let us turn now to the major administrative responsibilities churches face with regard to money. Here we shall consider ten.

1. Develop adequate perspective about money.
2. Develop a budget.
3. Anticipate sources of income.
4. Secure commitment to support the budget.
5. Use orderly plans for receiving the money.
6. Systematize the counting and banking.
7. Record monies received.
8. Use standard procedures for requisitioning, disbursing, and purchasing.
9. Use adequate accounting and auditing procedures.
10. Report appropriately to the church.

We shall examine each of these responsibilities and refer readers to more detailed help in other sources.

1. Develop an Adequate Perspective About Money

Effective administration of money in a church begins with developing an adequate perspective about money. This might very well be the most difficult part of the whole subject. Certainly it is the most abstract dimension of financial administration. It involves theological concepts. It reaches into the psychological. It affects the spiritual realm. It calls for a variety of skills. It surfaces in attitudes and behavior. It requires systematic, procedural attention and diligence. It is a very complex place at which to begin. But we have to begin there, and continue to work on this perspective as we deal with each of the other responsibilities. Let us elaborate about this adequate perspective we need to develop about money.

Many times some well-intended layperson has advised the pastor, usually a new pastor, that if the pastor would take care of the "spiritual," the laypeople would take care of the "temporal." In some instances the layperson no doubt meant to try to relieve the pastor of the burden of bothering with the finances. In other instances the layperson probably meant to advise the pastor to stay out of the church's financial business. Some have even told the pastor that he was not to preach about money. All of these notions, even those which were well-intended, represent inadequate perspectives about money.

Sometimes the most spiritual thing one might do is to manage money correctly. The spiritual and the temporal are too closely intertwined to be separated. The way a minister leads a church in its temporal affairs might be one of the strongest spiritual dimensions of all.

Jesus frequently referred to money.—Jesus spoke about stewardship of life more often than He spoke of any other subject. And He spoke about our relationships to money. It is not part of an adequate perspective regarding money to be silent about it. A constant stream of sermons or promotional emphases about money would be extreme in another inadequate direction. But it is right and healthy in a church to be open and realistic about money, and not as though it has no spiritual dimensions. It was the Lord Himself who said that where one's treasure is, there one's heart will be also. We do people a favor when we help them to develop their perspective and their values along the lines of Jesus' teachings. This applies to money as it does to other aspects of life.

There are other viewpoints about which some members might need to grow and develop. For example, it helps if the members understand that money isn't *everything*. It won't solve every problem. But, on the other hand, it is *something*, and it can help solve some problems. And it is not unspiritual to be open and realistic when money is being discussed.

A Christian view of material things is basic.—A Christian view of material things is part of an adequate perspective that helps in the administration of a church's finances. Members' support of the ministries of the church is another area. So is the matter of adequate provisions for the care of those who serve as ministers. Members' life-styles, especially with regard to the disposition of material goods above what is required to live with meaning as a Christian, is still another. On subjects like these you can spend years helping your people to grow in their understanding and practices. And as they grow, the finances of the church will likely be administered more effectively!

Lead church members to develop an adequate perspective about money.—Include appropriate messages—sermons— that will develop their perspective. Plan with the church's stewardship through the year. Some of these stewardship emphases should be directly related to money. Have members share authentic testimonies about their experiences in stewardship and finance. Relate the church's financial procedures, all the way from budget planning to the final reports to the members, to the theological, spiritual roots which justify the attention given to money. Celebrate what God is enabling the church to do through money and its proper use to fulfill the purpose of the church! An adequate perspective is essential to effective financial administration.

2. Develop a Budget

The second major responsibility in financial administration in a church is the development of a budget. *A budget is a comprehensive financial plan that reflects the specific amounts of money allocated from anticipated income for supporting the church's ministries and related expenses for a definite period of time, usually a year.* In some instances churches project their budgets over a period of several years into the future. In other instances churches budget by intervals within a year, such as quarterly or biannually. Again, the most common period of time for budgets is an annual budget. A church needs a budget to encourage proper direction, control, and accountability for its financial operation.

The line-item budget is most common.—The most common type of budget is what is called the line-item budget. In this kind of budget there is an allocation for each type of item for which there is anticipated expenditure, without regard for the particular activity or ministry the item supports. For example, all items of a particular kind like postage, literature, salaries, missions, benevolence, paper, socials, missions, would be listed, with possibly no more explanation than what I've given. Then an amount indicating the estimated expenditures would be listed opposite each item. Some have called this an accountant's format. It is fairly simple. Such a budget can be put together quickly. The previous year's budget, plus some projected adjustments up or down in estimates related to each item, would give you the new budget.

Many churches have been satisfied to use the line-item budget process. The *Church Finance Record System Manual* by Marvin Crowe and Merrill Moore gives excellent help for a church using the line-item budget. This manual was published by Broadman Press in 1959.

Ministry-action budgeting is growing in use.—There is another type of budget that is growing in popularity among churches. It is called ministry-action budgeting. Ministry-action budgeting is described in several publications prepared by stewardship leaders in state conventions and in the Southern Baptist Convention. The book, *Christian Stewardship in Action,* and the booklet, "Ministry Action Budgeting" gives excellent information about the process.

In ministry-action budgeting the budget takes the shape of major church programs. Budget requests as related to church programs are arranged according to their estimated priority in meeting needs compatible with the church's purpose and objectives. This system leads the church to think of the budget as a prioritized package of ministry actions to be carried out by the church. Members can see what ministry actions are proposed and how much money each costs. They can evaluate the ministry proposals, prepare the budget so that it reflects the proposed ministry actions and their costs, and present the budget to the church. This process means that the church adopts the plans for ministry along with the budget. Regular reports to the church follow the same lines—what ministries have been performed, and what the cost is for each ministry.

Steps in ministry-action budgeting.—These steps are to be followed in ministry-action budgeting:[2]

1. *Prepare Ministry Proposals*—The key instrument in ministry-action budgeting is the case-proposal made by every program or ministry of the church. The preparation of this

case-proposal (usually one page, as seen in Figure 1) is the
beginning step in budgeting and should include:
   a. a description of the purpose of the program and an
      indication as to how this supports the church's basic
      purpose;
   b. an identification of the needs that are to be met by this
      action and the benefits that are to come to the church;
   c. a list of things to be done next year (reachable goals);
   d. the cost in detail, not in lump sums;
   e. the long-range implication of the program (where this
      program will lead the church in three years, five years,
      and so forth, what it might cost in three years, five
      years; what it will be expected to accomplish in the
      future);
   f. an evaluation of possible alternates.
2. *Evaluate Program Proposals*—The second step in budgeting is to evaluate the priority of each program. Merit or
   priority should be assigned in terms of the church's purpose and goals by asking these questions.
   a. To what degree does this program make a contribution
      to the purpose of the church?
   b. What help will it be in assisting the church to reach its
      major objectives (goals)?
   c. Is this program needed any longer, or is there an alter-
      nate or better way to do this task?
   d. If the church should project this program, where will
      it lead the church in future years, and what will be its
      cost?
   e. Is there a program waiting to be included that is better,
      but excluded because of this program?
3. *Prepare the Budget*—Putting the programs together into
   a budget is the next step. It is good to let the format of the
   budget clearly reflect that it is a budget-of-programs,
   showing what is to be done and what it is going to cost.
4. *Present the Budget to the Church*—When the church is
   asked to discuss and finally vote, it is extremely important
   that the program be presented, as well as the amount of
   money involved. The act of approving a budget is also
   then an act of approving the programs of work.

Figure 1

A Ministry Action Proposal

For_____   Subject_____

1. A description of proposed plan and how it relates to the church's basic purpose.

_____

_____

_____

2. Why this ministry is needed. _____

_____

_____

_____

3. The costs to the church (in detail)._____

_____

_____

_____

4. What this will mean to the church in opportunities and cost in 2, 3, 5 years.

_____

_____

_____

5. Alternative. _____

_____

_____

_____

_____

6. Alternative. _____

_____

_____

_____

For every plan proposed there are alternatives. They are very important to the budget committee because they give variables for making judgments between one ministry and another.

5. *Promote the Budget*—Members should be asked to give to the support of this budget-of-programs. Again, this step in budgeting is distinguished by the accent on the program. It is not a case of raising money to meet or subscribe the budget; it is a case of support for the programs of work. Budget shortages are then considered program shortages or failures, and budget averages are seen as opportunities to do more in the programs of work.
6. *Report on the Budget*—The monthly report should be a program progress report. It should reflect:
   a. money given and how it was used in support of programs;
   b. progress in the program goals (for example, a monthly report could be a combined money report and program report);
   c. creative and varied techniques that help people understand and grow in interest.

There is a temptation to take the shortcut in budgeting. There are much easier ways to get a budget together than the proposal just offered. However, the test is not, "How little time and effort did it take?" but "How valuable is it to the future of the church?" It is important to understand that while ministry-action budgeting claims the prime virtue of making the church more aware of its purpose, the approach does not give up the needed controls of good financial procedures.

The Flow Chart in Figure 2 portrays this process of ministry-action budgeting. A minimum of ten weeks is required to adequately develop, prepare, and present a ministry budget.

Weeks Before Adoption	Step #	
10	1	Analyze ministries available to church. Elect a budget committee.
8	2	Show filmstrip, "Ministry Action Budgeting." Pre-

Figure 2

Flow Chart

Steps That Make Ministry-Action Budgeting a Simple Committee Procedure.

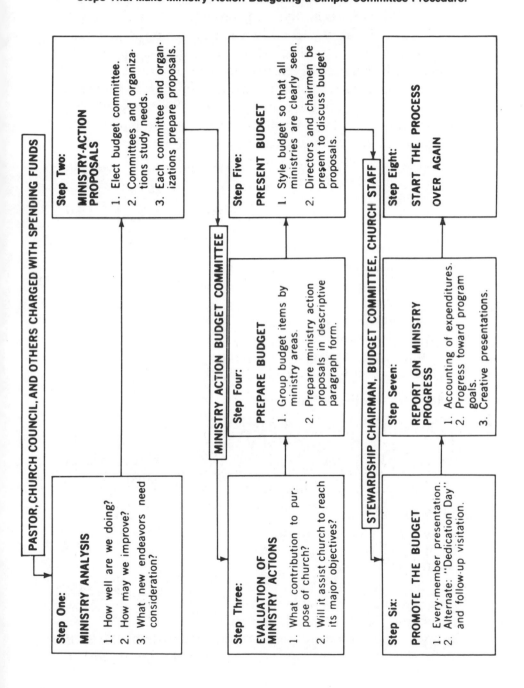

PASTOR, CHURCH COUNCIL, AND OTHERS CHARGED WITH SPENDING FUNDS

MINISTRY ACTION BUDGET COMMITTEE

STEWARDSHIP CHAIRMAN, BUDGET COMMITTEE, CHURCH STAFF

Step One:
MINISTRY ANALYSIS
1. How well are we doing?
2. How may we improve?
3. What new endeavors need consideration?

Step Two:
MINISTRY-ACTION PROPOSALS
1. Elect budget committee.
2. Committees and organizations study needs.
3. Each committee and organizations prepare proposals.

Step Three:
EVALUATION OF MINISTRY ACTIONS
1. What contribution to purpose of church?
2. Will it assist church to reach its major objectives?

Step Four:
PREPARE BUDGET
1. Group budget items by ministry areas.
2. Prepare ministry action proposals in descriptive paragraph form.

Step Five:
PRESENT BUDGET
1. Style budget so that all ministries are clearly seen.
2. Directors and chairmen be present to discuss budget proposals.

Step Six:
PROMOTE THE BUDGET
1. Every-member presentation.
2. Alternate: "Dedication Day" and follow-up visitation.

Step Seven:
REPORT ON MINISTRY PROGRESS
1. Accounting of expenditures.
2. Progress toward program goals.
3. Creative presentations.

Step Eight:
START THE PROCESS OVER AGAIN

		pare ministry-action proposals.
5		Proposal hearing by budget committee.
4	3	Evaluate proposals and set priorities.
3	4	Prepare budget for distribution.
1	5	Present and discuss ministry budget.
	6	Ministry Adoption Day.

Church leaders might wish to experiment with ministry-action budgeting. It offers far more motivational potential than does the line-item budget. Ministry-action budgeting informs the members more in terms of their interest. Church members could be very interested in what is being accomplished in ministry and at what cost. One good experience with ministry-action budgeting probably would convince church leaders of its value as a tool for financial administration.

3. Anticipate Sources of Income

A third major administrative responsibility in church finance is to anticipate the sources of income for the church. It is important to know how much money the church might reasonably expect to receive during the period to be covered by the new budget. A major part of the work of those who plan the church budget is to estimate how much money might come in and from what sources it might be expected to come.

In many churches, most of the money can be expected to come from the undesignated tithes and offerings of the members. This source might be subdivided to reflect what comes through regular gifts in church offering envelopes, usually through the Sunday School, and that which comes as "loose offerings" in the offering plates during the worship services. Usually smaller proportions come as designated gifts for special causes. Other sources for some churches include rental fees from properties, memorial gifts, interest income on money invested, trusts, wills, refunds of money from vending machines and from meals served at the church, capital gifts, and other sources.

The usual way of estimating the income for the next year is to study the patterns of giving for previous years and project the trend into the future. The projection might be the anticipated percentage increase, translated to actual dollars. Other factors might enter into the projection, such as the state of the economy where the church is located and anticipated changes in the membership of the church.

Program planners should lead in allocation changes.—It is possible that some changes might need to be made in the plans for ministry after the income is anticipated for the coming budget period. If changes are needed, *be sure to let those who planned the programs determine which ones should be adjusted or deleted.* Don't put that responsibility on your budget planners. Let them confine their attention to budget planning, not program planning to the exclusion of the leaders of the church programs. The same principle applies to adjustments in compensation for the church staff. Let the church personnel committee determine, subject to church approval, the compensation changes for church staff members. Do not put that burden on budget planners!

Avoid legally or ethically questionable money-making projects.—One concern about sources of church income might warrant being mentioned here. A practice seems to be growing rapidly among churches, and it needs some careful thought by church leaders and members. That is the practice of money-making projects to support church ministries. Service projects like car washes, merchandising goods through sales campaigns, on-premises garage sales, and the like raise for some both legal and ethical questions for a church. The legal area involves tax laws and possibly license violations. The ethical area includes whether a normally tax-exempt church should enter into business activities which could be perceived to be in competition with others who deal in the same commodities or services.

In many communities there is a generous attitude toward

churches which allows the concerns about such "minor" legal or ethical questions to be overlooked. Many church members, though, probably would rather increase their gifts than to jeopardize the good and right standing of the churches. We cannot go into all the aspects of the question here, but church leaders should carefully think through this problem and try to find ways to fund church ministries that don't violate legal or ethical considerations for the church! We should do this because it is right. And we also need to be in a position to defend the church in an increasingly hostile environment from the strongest position we can secure.

4. Secure Commitment to Support the Budget

The fourth responsibility in administering church finances is to secure commitment of the members to support the budget. There are at least half a dozen ways for which there are denominational materials available to help a church in securing commitment of the members to support the budget. Helpful materials are available through the Southern Baptist Convention Stewardship Services, 901 Commerce Street, Nashville, Tennessee 37203.

Here are six ways from which church leaders might choose to lead church members to support the budget. One is called "The Forward Program." It requires eight weeks to prepare and present, including a four-Sunday emphasis. Next is the "Alternate Forward Program," which requires six weeks to prepare and present, including a three-Sunday emphasis. Third is a plan called "Committed to Ministries." This plan requires eight weeks to prepare and present, including a three-Sunday emphasis. Fourth is a "Tithers Commitment Program," which takes four weeks to prepare and present, including a two-Sunday emphasis. Fifth is a "Stewardship Revival." The time required for preparing and presenting the stewardship revival is four weeks, including a two-Sunday emphasis. The sixth plan is called "Simplified Church Budget Development and Promotion," which calls for two weeks of preparation and presentation, including a two-Sunday emphasis.

Church leaders should obtain sample materials for the kinds

of emphases they wish to consider. Then they should compare the various program features and choose the one that best suits the needs and readiness of the church. Generally speaking, these plans produce results in keeping with the effort put into them. With some experimenting, leaders can determine what is best for a particular church in getting the members to support the financial plan.

5. Use Orderly Plans for Receiving the Money

The fifth administrative responsibility is having orderly plans for receiving the money for the church. The plan should include decisions about using standard envelopes for members' gifts. Income is definitely increased with the use of envelopes. And there are some choices to be made regarding size, color, and manner of distributing the envelopes to the members. Other parts of an adequate plan deal with the system of collecting the offerings, both those that involve the use of envelopes and those that come in other forms.

Any plan needs to afford maximum security for collecting the offering envelopes during Sunday School. Church leaders need to develop a simple standard procedure which includes leaving all envelopes sealed until they reach the point where the official money counters work.

There should be a consistent plan for handling the money received in offering plates during worship services. Do the collectors (ushers, deacons, others) bring the offering plates to the offering table with or without the money still in them? Where does the money stay until it gets to the official counters? Who is responsible for transferring the money to the counters? These and other questions need to be answered in an adequate plan to fulfill this responsibility of appropriately receiving the money.

6. Systematize Counting and Banking

A sixth area for administrative attention is counting and banking the church's money. Who will count the money? A committee of no less than three should count the money, although, unfortunately, in most churches one person could actually do the counting. Churches should avoid having a member count the money alone and be open to question as to his or her integrity. Too, it is wise to reduce any temptation at this point. Leaders must use extreme care as they change from a one-person system of counting, banking, or other aspects of handling church funds.

When will the money be counted? Some counting committees work during the worship services. Others count just after each service. Others come later in the day or even on another day to count. Where will the money rest if there is a delay in counting? And where will the actual counting take place? What procedures will the counting committee follow? These should be written out in checklist fashion and followed without fail. How will you reconcile differences in amounts entered on the outside of offering envelopes and the amounts enclosed in the envelopes? There are suggestions for all of these questions in materials supplied by the Stewardship Commission of the Southern Baptist Convention or in the book by Moore and Crowe mentioned earlier.

There are important decisions to make about banking the church's money. Who makes the actual deposits? Where will they be made? When will the money be deposited? Will it be counted before it is deposited, or will it be left in locked bags at the bank for later counting at the bank? Or will it be brought back to the church for counting? How many people will accompany the money to and from the bank? Do you need professional security personnel to transport the money? In many churches both the people who handle the money and the money itself are covered by insurance. The people are of more value than the money, and potential threats to their security should be minimized by good procedures.

7. Record Monies Received

The seventh area for administrative leadership involves recording the gifts and other receipts. The possibilities range from posting individual gifts by hand to machine posting and on to electronic data processing by computer. A demonstration of the range of computer services, including financial record keeping, which are presently available to churches almost everywhere could be most helpful to church leaders.

Whatever method is used to record members' gifts, the records should be faithfully and accurately kept. Members should receive copies of the record of their gifts, at least annually and preferably each quarter. The shorter interval allows any corrections in the records to be made before the facts get too cold. Assurance that gifts actually reach their intended destinations is important beyond words to members' confidence in the church's handling of money.

8. Use Standard Procedures for Requisitioning, Disbursing, and Purchasing

The eighth area of administrative responsibility in church finance is requisitioning, disbursing, and purchasing. It is helpful for a church to have a simple but standard form on which written requests, called requisitions, for items which require money are made. This enables the person who is responsible to verify that the item is anticipated in the budget and that there is money available for it at the time requested. Normally, it is not that person's prerogative to deny the request if it is approved in the budget *and* if there is presently money available to cover the expenditure. When all is in order regarding the requisition, the money can be disbursed for cash purchases, or the purchase can be charged to the church's account for later payment following billing.

The procedures for purchasing need to be determined in a church. It needs to be clear just who is authorized to purchase and how this person is to go about it. Questions about purchasing in volume need to be considered. Considerable savings can sometimes be realized by buying items which are used in large quantity in larger volumes. Then, of course, come other questions such as whether or not there is satisfactory storage and distribution for these items. There are other matters leaders need to work out regarding purchasing. One important matter is to verify that what is received is exactly what was ordered. Other matters include buying wholesale or retail, paying with the order but before receiving the goods purchased, whether to maintain a limit like a thirty-day period following billing for payment to be made, and many others.

9. Use Adequate Accounting and Auditing Procedures

Accounting and auditing is the ninth area for administrative attention in church finance. The book by Moore and Crowe, *Church Finance Record System Manual*, or other materials available from the Stewardship Commission offer practical help. Leaders can adapt and adopt a system that is tailored to the church's accounting needs.

Moore and Crowe give a sample procedure which a church audit committee can use to perform an audit of the church's records and finances. An annual audit is recommended, and it should be done by persons who are not involved in handling the church's money or in purchasing or bookkeeping for the church. A committee whose members can do simple arithmetic can perform the audit for the majority of churches. Larger churches might need to pay for a professional audit. This examination and verification of accounts should be routine. It should not come only when there is concern about some problem in a church's finances. It is far more valuable to prevent problems than to uncover them after some unfortunate experience.

10. Report Appropriately to the Church

The tenth administrative responsibility in church finance is reporting. Church leaders should inform members of income, expenditures, variances, adjustments, and special opportunities, needs, or problems related to the church's finances. Most churches require a monthly report to the church in a business meeting. Some have only quarterly reports. Almost all churches then have an annual financial report. These reports usually follow the format of the church budget. They show ministry-by-ministry or item-by-item what was allocated during the reporting period and what was spent. Some reports are given in great detail, and include the percentages figures represent, how the present report compares with the report for the same time last year, and many other items of information.

How much to report is a matter for each church to determine. In general, it is better to give a bit more than is required than to give less and thereby arouse suspicion that something might be wrong in the finances.

The administration of a church's financial resources is a very important and sometimes complex area. A church needs the help of a good number of faithful people to see that the finances are well administered. Money is not a worthy end in itself. It is a necessary means to other ends. In a church, the end desired is to help the church to fulfill its purpose.

Summary

Good administrative leadership with financial resources in a church is vital. Financial resources make up a vital link in the ministry chain. They help to make available the physical resources and support the human resources in performing a church's ministries. Financial resources includes more than money, but money is the focus of the administrative ideas in this chapter.

There are numerous major areas of responsibility in administering financial resources. In this chapter we have described ten areas related to money in the church and offered some key suggestions about them. The first area is probably the most important: develop an adequate perspective about money. The other nine are mostly procedural and can be done well only if the first one is in working order.

Learning Activity Suggestions

1. List the major points, in your own words, which express what you think make up an adequate perspective about money in a church. For each of these suggest at least one approach you would recommend for implementation with a congregation.

2. Secure copies of the monthly financial reports of five churches, including at least one that uses ministry-action budgeting in its format. Compare these budgets, looking for strengths, weaknesses, and ideas new to you.

3. Review numbers five through ten of the responsibility areas regarding money in the church. Select one area, and write a one-page sample procedure for dealing effectively in this area.

Notes

1. For excellent help in developing an adequate perspective about money, see these two books by Cecil Ray:
   Living the Responsible Life (Nashville: Convention Press, 1974).
   How to Specialize in Christian Living (Nashville: Convention Press, 1982); and
   Lee E. Davis, *In Charge: Managing Money for Christian Living* (Nashville: Broadman Press, 1984).
2. Charles A. Tidwell, "Administering Educational Support Services," *Christian Education Handbook*, Bruce P. Powers, ed./comp. (Nashville: Broadman Press, 1981), pp. 212-216.

9
Providing Administrative Control

Whatever your task, work heartily, as serving the Lord and not men, knowing that from the Lord you will receive the inheritance as your reward; you are serving the Lord Christ (Col. 3:23-24, RSV).

Ideas This Chapter Includes

The concept of control

Control in a church

Instruments used to control

In this text we have described the church as a body of those who have received Christ and who are trying together to live His way and to work with Him in the redemptive enterprise. We have identified the church as a fellowship. We have referred to it as an organism, a unit of life. We have shown the ways the church can be intentional as it tries to be the church, and to do the work of a church.

Early in this volume we define church administration as enabling the children of God who make up the church to become and to do all they can become and do, by God's grace. We have spent entire chapters elaborating on how leaders must lead a church to clarify its purpose, determine its objectives, develop ministry plans, design organization to implement the plans, and administer human, physical, and financial resources.

One major area remains for our consideration of the functional areas of church administration. It is the area which deals with such questions as, How can a church accurately keep up with what it is accomplishing? How can a church give direction to its activities in ways that keep the activities on track toward the intended outcomes? How can a church compare its progress with its plans, and apply as necessary the corrective measures so that performance takes place according to the plans? What are the instruments a church might use to give administrative guidance as it moves toward its objective and fulfills its purpose?

In much of the literature of administration this area is called "administrative controls." Lemke and Edwards defined administrative control as "the review of actual progress by comparison with the plan and observation of the variance or deviation."[1] Gordon R. Terry defined it as "determining what is being accomplished, that is, evaluating the performance and, if necessary, applying corrective measures so that the performance takes place according to plan."[2] How can a church do this? That is what this chapter is about.

Through studying this chapter the reader should understand better what control in a church means. Beyond understanding, it is hoped that the reader will know some of the instruments or means which one could use in a church and something of how to use them to help the church fulfill its purpose.

Concept of Control

Let us look first at the concept of control. It is very important to see control in an accurate and positive way. For that reason, some like the alternate term *administrative guidance.* This is a more active and positive term, whereas control seems more passive and negative. The truth is that there might be some of all these attributes involved in control or administrative guidance: active, passive, positive, and negative.

Experience Increases Appreciation for Controls

Leaders come to appreciate controls when they have some experience in which something gets out of control. An illustration from my youth makes the point clear. I was the youngest of several boys in a large family. Our family car was a 1930 Model A Ford. One good reason that car served as our family transportation for more than twenty-three years was that my father kept the only set of keys and was its only operator. Now, that in itself is a kind of control, but that is not the point of the story.

When I came home for the summer following my sophomore year in college, I worked as the director of a new city playground. I needed transportation for at least two round trips daily across town. I also needed storage space for an assortment of equipment. The Model A Ford was just right for both needs. Since the car was already twenty-one years old, my father gave in to my request to be allowed to use it, even though it was the only car in the family.

Everything went very nicely until one afternoon as I made my way across town after having enjoyed a good lunch of my mother's home cooking. I routinely stopped for a traffic light at the top of a hill on a four-lane thoroughfare. When the light turned green I started down the hill in the lane next to the center stripes in the street. Suddenly I noticed that the steering wheel did not respond properly to my touch. The car began to head into the lanes where normally there was a stream of oncoming traffic. Providentially, there was not another car in sight for several blocks. This only slightly relieved my confusion and near panic. I turned the steering wheel to the right. The car went to the left! I applied the brakes, and found them in good shape (thank heaven!). But when I did that, the car did a left turn so sharp that it soon came to rest with both front wheels perpendicular to the curb on the wrong side of the street! I was not injured. The car had only minor damage.

What had gone wrong? The tie rod that causes the car wheels to respond to the turning of the steering wheel had become worn and had disconnected suddenly and without warning. When I had wanted so very desperately to have control of the direction of the car, it was almost absolutely out of control. What an appreciation I came to have for control!

There are controls in a car other than the steering wheel. The accelerator and the brakes are control devices. In limited ways, the curbs on the streets also serve as boundaries or controls. All of these control devices are important and necessary. But the most significant control is the steering mechanism.

Organizations Need Controls

An organization that is on the move needs control—guidance—just as surely as does an automobile. You might need ways to accelerate or decelerate to govern the speed. You might need ways to put on the brakes. You could at times need curbs to effectively mark boundaries. You certainly need ways to get information about the movement or the condition of the church. Most important, you need ways to steer the church as it moves on its course. It is for such needs as these that we recommend good administrative guidance, good controls.

Control in a Church

A church has the responsibility and the right to establish and to execute its controls. These controls should be designed and used so as to represent the will of the church as a body and not the will of any one person or group within a church. Often a church might designate one person or several to be responsible for seeing that the controls are properly administered. But, ultimately, we are advocating controls which are those of the church as a body, the body of Christ. We are not advocating the kind of domineering individual or small group control that takes from a church its responsibility and right to guide and govern itself under Christ. Simply put, the concept of controls we advocate is one that provides for the church positive steering mechanism that enable the whole body to function according to its intentions and desires.

Let us look now at some of the instruments or means that might be useful in giving administrative guidance or controls for a church. There are several ways of viewing these instruments. In fact, some of the means we shall suggest might be excluded from the lists of others.

The noted management consultant and author, Edward C. Schleh, suggested that you begin and end control in an enterprise by controlling "the man." If you control your individual personnel, you can control the rest of the operation. He builds a strong case for this view.[3]

Charles Hickman Titus, whose book *The Processes of Leadership* is a classic in the field of political leadership, identified two points of control as those which are the minimum essential for controlling any organization. Titus said that you must control the leader selection process, and you must control the platform.[4] Translating the platform from the political realm, it becomes for the church the proposed ministry plans. Titus has certainly identified two very basic items related to control in a church. His approach is political by design. Still, church leaders can learn from him. Leader selection and ministry planning are vital points for control in a church.

Tools for Control in the Functional
Areas of Administration

For our purposes of studying controls in the church we shall use the administrative areas that identify the *means* of administration. In each of these administrative areas we shall suggest several possible tools or instruments for steering or controlling. Specifically, we shall consider the areas of developing ministry plans, designing organization, administering human resources, physical resources, and financial resources.

In all of these areas there are certain approaches or factors which are essential to the kind of control we are advocating. These approaches or factors are themselves in some instances instruments of control: democratic procedures of decision making; policies; operating procedures; standards; evaluation; and communication. Keep these in mind as we consider some suggested ways of providing guidance.

A Plan for Planning Helps a Church
Control Its Ministries

In the administrative area of developing ministry plans, a church should exercise guidance through having a plan for planning. This plan for planning should be no secret. It should, in effect, be a known procedure for getting a ministry event or emphasis on the church's agenda. It should clarify the route a person or a group should follow to place an event or an entire program in the church's ministry plan. Usually this plan for planning would include presentation to the Church Council. It might also involve organizational councils or church committees. At times a member of the church or the church staff might originate the idea for ministry.

A church needs control of its ministry planning, and a plan for planning could provide what is needed. Positively, members and groups need to know how ministries come to have church support. A plan for planning should require answers in advance as to what is proposed, when, where, for whom and by whom, how, and at what expense. If curriculum materials, these would be determined in the plan. Figure 1 suggests the kind of items which a given plan for planning might include.

Church Calendar Is a Ministry Control Tool

Related also to developing ministry plans, the church calendar serves as a control or guidance device. Someone should be designated to be the official keeper of the church calendar. Members and groups need instructions about how to have an item entered properly in the church calendar.

Control Devices Related to Organization

In the area of designing the organization, there are certain devices which are useful as guidance tools. Most useful are a church constitution and bylaws, an organization design procedure, organizational charts, and lists of organizational components. (See Appendix A for a sample constitution and bylaws.)

A Church Needs to Control Organization Design

As indicated in the chapter on organization, a church's organization design should flow out of its purpose, objectives, and its program. Each program organization should initiate the design for its work. The Sunday School would create an organization design for each coming year in consultation with departmental leaders and teachers as to the organizational needs in various age groups. Church staff members related to the program should assist and advise regarding the organization design. Changes during the year should be similarly planned. This council should inform the Church Council, the church nominating committee, and other related groups as to the changes in organization which impact their work. Proven organizational patterns should prevail where possible, with ex-

Figure 1
Suggested Design Procedure for Developing a
Church Program or Event

1. Identify purpose

2. Determine objectives

3. Develop program/event
   a. Set goals to meet needs
   b. List activities/projects
   c. Plan actions: schedules; locations

4. Design organization

5. Secure human resources
   a. Enlist and train leaders
   b. Recruit members
   c. Plan for supervision of a and b
   d. Involve in further development of program

6. Provide physical resources
   a. Select curriculum materials; other materials
   b. Reserve meeting place(s)
   c. Arrange for equipment/furnishings

7. Allocate financial resources
   a. Identify sources
   b. Secure commitment; allocations

8. Design promotion plans; assign

9. Establish Controls
   a. Records
   b. Reports
   c. Policies
   d. Procedures
   e. Coordinate

10. Evaluate
    a. Secure pertinent date
    b. Compare with goals
    c. Note items for future reference
    d. Communicate evaluation as useful

perimental designs clearly identified as experimental, and given a reasonable time and effort to prove their value. Generally, experimental designs should be tried successfully on a limited and controlled scale before their installation as the dominant design.

Church Staff and Volunteers Need Controls

In the administrative area of human resources there are numerous controls. The list includes job qualifications, job descriptions, leader selection and recruitment procedures, staff meetings, workers' meetings, supervision, work schedules, worker development/training, performance reviews, and compensation plans. Each of these contributes to the guidance "mechanism" in a church. The sample job description for a minister of education shown in Figure 2 serves to illustrate the instruments that could serve the human resources area. As indicated in the chapter on human resources, the church personnel committee should lead in providing the administrative controls instruments as related to the church staff. The church nominating committee should lead in relating to volunteer workers with the assistance of appropriate church staff members.

A Church Benefits by Controlling Its Physical Resources

The administrative area of physical resources requires several control tools in order to be most effective. There need to be plans, policies and/or procedures for procuring things like materials, equipment, furnishings, and supplies. Distribution and use plans, and in some instances, an inventory system are needed. Inspection procedures are another helpful control. Increasingly, churches are needing to develop more adequate security plans to protect their physical goods. And, as in other areas, records and reports are parts of useful control. Figures 3 through 8 illustrate useful control forms for physical resources.

Financial Resources Require Numerous Controls

In the area of financial administration the budgeting process and the budget itself are tools for administrative control.

Figure 2
Sample Job Description
Minister of Education

Principle Function:

Responsible to the church for leadership in an effective church ministry of religious education.

Supervised by:

The pastor.

Responsibilities:

1. Lead in planning the church's educational ministries in ways that advance the fulfillment of the church's purpose and objectives, and meet the needs of church and community.

2. Lead in organizing the educational ministries.

3. Lead in providing adequate personnel, both volunteer and staff, for the educational ministries.

4. Lead in providing suitable physical resources for the educational ministries.

5. Lead in providing sufficient financial resources for the educational ministries.

6. Lead in applying administrative controls related to the educational ministries.

7. Lead in securing attendance and participation in the educational ministries.

8. Work cooperatively with the pastor, other staff members, and the church members regarding the total church ministries; and with other bodies in essentially mutual endeavors.

9. Continue personal growth in knowledge, skills, spiritual development, and churchmanship.

There should also be procedures for receiving, counting, banking, and recording the receipts. The following suggestions from J. M. Crowe and Merrill D. Moore are excellent directions for these needs.[5]

Procedures for receiving funds.—It is extremely important from both a moral and a business viewpoint that a church handle all its receipts carefully and accurately. Procedures should be adopted which will guarantee the safety of the money and its use according to the will of the donor. Such procedures should provide adequate protection against criticism of church officers who handle the funds.

Use of individual offering envelopes.—The Church Finance Record System assumes that each member of the church and Sunday School will be given a package of church offering envelopes. The system also assumes that each person will bring that offering in his or her envelope to the first service which they attend each Sunday. Each person should be encouraged to use his or her own numbered and dated envelope. However, a supply of bulk envelopes should be kept at the church for use by visitors and by members who forget to bring their own envelopes.

A definite procedure for receiving envelopes.—Most of the envelopes will be received in the Sunday School classes. The class secretary (or adult worker in preschool and children's departments) will post each member's record to the appropriate record forms but will not open any envelopes. If any envelope does not have an amount written upon it, the class secretary will not include this envelope in compiling the class record contributions.

The class secretary should deliver the class report and all offering envelopes to the department secretary, who will prepare the report for the department but will not open any envelopes. The department secretary should deliver the department report to the general secretary and all the offering envelopes to the counting committee. Each department should be furnished a money bag or other container for bringing the envelopes to the counting committee. The counting committee should have a room equipped with tables and chairs, if possible.

Counting committee.—The counting committee should be elected by the church. It should have a large enough membership so that at least two members could always assist in counting the money. In some churches, the counting committee is divided into teams, each team taking its turn in a rotating plan by Sundays or by months.

The counting committee should receive the envelopes from the Sunday School department secretaries. They may gather the offering into bags to be placed in the safe or in a night depository for later counting, or they may count it as they receive it. Whenever the counting is done, the following steps are recommended.

1. Separate all loose offerings, if any, from the envelopes. Count the loose offering and enter the amount on the Summary of Receipts.

2. Open each envelope, remove the money or check from the envelope, and verify the amount taken from the envelope with the amount written on the envelope. If there is any discrepancy or if the figures are not legible, write the correct amount on the envelope and circle it to indicate that a correction has been made by the counting committee. If the difference between the amount enclosed and the amount written on the envelope is significant, it is wise to talk with the contributor as soon as possible. The total offering of a family is sometimes enclosed in one envelope and the amounts entered on the envelopes of several members of the family. Perhaps the simplest way to handle this problem is to lay aside all envelopes of that family until the amounts marked balance with the cash enclosed.

3. Separate the budget offering envelopes from the special offering envelopes. Add the budget offering envelopes and enter the total on the Summary of Receipts. Add the special offering envelopes and enter the totals on the Summary of Receipts. If an adding machine is not available to the counting committee, the envelopes may be arranged by the amounts given to make addition easier. That is, envelopes for those giving one dollar may be placed together and counted and so forth.

Figure 3

Request for Facilities, Equipment and Supplies

Organization of Groups_____

Activity_____ Approximate Attendance at Activity_____

Date of Activity _____ Time _____

FACILITIES AND EQUIPMENT NEEDED (Rooms, chairs, tables, visual aids, etc.)_____
_____

KITCHEN NEEDS (Food, supplies, etc.)_____
_____

NURSERY AND CHILD CARE (List the number of children by ages)
_____ 1 yr. & below_____ 2 & 3 years_____ 4 & 5 years_____
6 to 8 years_____ 9 to 12 years

Diagram Special Room Arrangement Below

Requested by_____ Date Requested_____
ALL DATES MUST RECEIVE FINAL APPROVAL AT THE
WEEKLY CALENDAR MEETING ON TUESDAY

RETURN ALL COPIES TO BUSINESS OFFICE

NOTE: In addition to the original, there should be copies for house-keeping, kitchen, and child care personnel.

Figure 4

Inspection Report
(To Be Used By Property and Space Committee)

Date _____ Time _____ a.m.
_____ p.m. Inspected by _____

Indicate Condition By: Clean, Dirty, Good, or Bad

Room	Floor	Walls	Ceiling	Woodwork	Windows	Plumbing	Hardware	Lights	Remarks

Recommendations:

Figure 5

PIANO
Maintenance and Tuning Schedule

A Yearly Maintenance Contract Is Recommended for Piano and Organ Tuning.

Brand Name, Serial No. and Location	Date Purchased and Cost	Date Last Tuned	Remarks

Figure 6

Special Work Request

Attention: _____

Will you please fulfill the following request—

_____

_____

_____

_____

_____

Room _____   Work Completed By:

Date Needed _____   _____

Time Needed _____   Date_____Time_____

Requested By _____

Equipment Record

Serial or
Item _____   Identification No._____

Location _____

Date Purchased _____ Cost _____

Name and Address of Seller _____

_____

Person to Call for Service:

Name_____Phones_____

Date On Needed Maintenance _____

_____

Record of Servicing

Date	Servicing Company	Type of Service Performed	Cost
_____	_____	_____	_____
_____	_____	_____	_____
_____	_____	_____	_____

—Continue Servicing Record On Back Side

Figure 7

Food Service Request

_____
(Date)

To: Church Business Office

From: _____

Type of Service_____Date_____Hour_____

To Be Served In _____

Organization to be served _____

Individual Requesting Service _____

Number to be served _____

Budget Item to be charged, if any, _____

    Additional materials and/or supplies needed:

_____

_____

_____

_____

_____

_____

    Request Approved:

_____

    Please draw a sketch of how you want the tables arranged for your program. Indicate the location of the head table and the number of tables you desire. Each table will seat four people on each side.

Figure 8

Rest Room Cleaning Checklist

Month_____ Rest Room No. or Location_____

Put check under item on day cleaned

	Receptacles Emptied*	Toilet Tissue Refilled*	Paper Towels Refilled*	Soap Refilled*	Lavatory Cleaned	Commode Cleaned & Disinfected	Mirror Cleaned	Floor Scrubbed	Deodorizer Checked	Walls Cleaned	Windows Cleaned	Hardware Cleaned	Plumbing Operating OK Yes or No	Remarks	Work Done
1															
2															
3															
4															
5															
6															
7															
8															
9															
10															
11															
12															
13															
14															
15															
16															
17															
18															
19															
20															
21															
22															
23															
24															
25															
26															
27															
28															
29															
30															
31															

*Items To Be Checked Daily
All Other Items to Be Done As Needed or At Least Once Each Week.

4. Count checks, currency, and coins and enter the total of each on the Summary of Receipts.

5. Add the cash items as entered in the first section of the Summary of Receipts and the sources of cash as entered in the second section. If these two totals do not balance, recheck both the cash and the envelopes. If they cannot be made to balance, enter the difference on the proper line near the bottom of the Summary of Receipts form.

6. The counters should then certify that the summary is correct by signing in the proper column.

Offerings should come to the counting committee.—After the offering is taken in the Sunday morning and evening worship services, it should be delivered to the counting committee. The counting committee should follow the same procedure in dealing with these offerings as with those received through the Sunday School. If checks are received which are not enclosed in envelopes, the counting committee should prepare envelopes for them.

The financial secretary or the church office may receive offerings during the week. In order to maintain good internal control, a triplicate receipt should be prepared for each person making such a contribution. The receipt should indicate the amount of the contribution and the purpose for which it was given. One copy of the receipt should be given or mailed to the person making the offering, one copy clipped to the offering, and the third copy should remain in the receipt book.

All money received during the preceding week and copies of all receipts written should be given to the counting committee on the following Sunday. The counting committee should use the same procedure in handling these funds as with the offerings received during the Sunday School.

The Summary of Receipts has five columns in order that the counting committee may record separately the funds received through the Sunday School, morning worship, evening worship, and during the preceding week. This type of summary provides an accurate and informative analysis of the receipts. However, some counting committees will prefer to count all funds received during all services each week at one time and to enter the entire record in the total column.

Counting committee should prepare the deposit.—When the envelopes have been opened and all counting and checking has been completed, the counting committee is ready to prepare the deposit. The following steps are suggested for preparing the deposit.

1. Place pennies, nickels, dimes, quarters, and half dollars in wrappers or tubes which may be secured without charge from local banks. Place the miscellaneous coins which are left over from the wrappers or tubes in an envelope and write on the envelope the amount enclosed. (Some banks have automatic machines for counting coins and prefer to have the coins unwrapped.)

2. Separate the currency according to denominations. Arrange with all bills facing in the same direction. Band each denomination with wrappers which may be obtained without charge from local banks.

3. Endorse all checks with the words *For Deposit Only* and the name of your church. A rubber stamp may be used to save time.

4. Enter the amount of coins, currency, and each check on a deposit ticket provided by the bank. The total amount of the deposit and the total amount of the receipts as entered on the Summary of Receipts must be in agreement. The deposit ticket should be prepared in duplicate. The bank will keep one copy and will receipt the duplicate copy.

5. The duplicate copy of the deposit ticket and one copy of the Summary of Receipts should be forwarded to the church treasurer immediately. The second copy of the Summary of Receipts, all offering envelopes, receipts, or other documents indicating source and/or pupose of funds should be delivered to the financial secretary. The third copy of the Summary of Receipts should be kept in a chronological file by the chairman of the counting committee.

Church treasurer records and files receipt information. —The treasurer should receive a copy of the Summary of Receipts and a duplicate copy of the bank deposit ticket each week from the counting committee. He should transfer the information from the Summary of Receipts to the cash receipts journal which provides a page for each month in the year.

After entering the information in the cash receipts journal, the treasurer should file the Summary of Receipts and the duplicate bank deposit ticket chronologically. The monthly bank statement may be placed in the same file.

At the end of the month, the treasurer should total the record of receipts for the entire month. This information will be needed for his or her monthly report to the church.

Internal control.—Some other aspects of financial control include internal control, procedures for disbursing funds, records, reports, and audits. Crowe and Moore have this to say about internal control:

1. Sunday School class, department, and general secretaries do not open any offering envelopes.

2. Church ushers do not open any envelopes.

3. All envelopes, loose plate offerings, designated offerings, and miscellaneous receipts are delivered to the counting committee, which is composed of at least three persons.

4. All errors are entered on the envelope or receipt and circled by the counting committee.

5. The counting committee prepares and makes the deposit in the bank. However, the counting committee does not enter the record of contributions or have anything to do with the disbursement of the funds.[6]

Church Finances Should Be Audited Regularly

The audit of church financial operations is probably one of the most neglected areas of financial control among churches. In view of this need, we present the following information, again drawing upon the Crowe and Moore manual.[7]

An audit is an examination by a disinterested party of the procedures used in handling cash receipts and disbursements and of the accounting records and reports.

The primary purposes of an audit of financial records are twofold: (1) to provide the church and its leadership with assurance that all funds have been handled according to the instruction of the church and (2) to provide an appraisal of the effectiveness with which the accounting responsibilities are being performed.

The church may elect an auditor from its membership who will serve without pay, or it may employ an auditor to do the work. Ideally, the auditor should have good knowledge of fund accounting and some experience in the examination of accounting records and report writing.

The auditor should:

1. Review the church's constitution and bylaws to discover instructions contained in them concerning the handling and use of funds.

2. Study the approved manuals or statements of procedure relating to the financial programs.

3. Examine the recorded minutes of the church indicating adoption of the budget, authorizing changes in the budget, and approving expenditures for items not included in the budget.

4. Examine the financial records including the file of offering envelopes, weekly Summary of Receipts, receipts journal, disbursements journal, cancelled checks, paid invoices, insurance records, property evaluations, reserve funds, bank accounts, and all other financial transactions.

Volunteer auditors. In recognition of the fact that many churches will not have access to personnel trained in audit procedures, the following methods are suggested:

I. Auditing for dollar accuracy:
   1. Spot check the offering envelopes to determine that the Summary of Receipts balances with their requirements.
   2. Verify deposits shown on monthly bank statements with the Summary of Receipts prepared by the counting committee each week.
   3. Verify the Summary of Receipts with the entries recorded in the receipts journal.
   4. Verify paid voucher file for proper approval for payment of all invoices.
   5. Verify paid vouchers with the disbursements journal for proper entry and distribution of charges to budget and designated fund accounts.

6. Check accuracy of footings in all journals.
7. Reconcile the bank statement and list outstanding checks and deposits.

II. Auditing approved procedures:
1. Determine if approved procedures have been followed in the handling of receipts and disbursements and in the preparation and presentation of reports.
2. Determine whether all undesignated funds have been expended according to the adopted budget or subsequent instruction of the church as recorded in the church minutes.
3. Determine if designated funds have been disbursed according to the instructions of the giver.
4. Study approval procedures to determine whether they provide sufficient internal control.

III. Auditing the insurance plan:
Review the insurance plan to determine if sufficient amounts of insurance are carried for property, personal liability, theft, bond, and so forth.

Auditor's Report

The auditor should complete his examination as soon as possible after the close of the fiscal (which is usally the calendar) year. He should aim at having his report ready within one month after the end of the year. The report should be made to the church.

The auditor's report should include:
1. A statement of the bylaws requiring the audit, if such bylaws exist;
2. A statement of the scope of the audit;
3. A statement of findings and recommendations, if any;
4. A reconciliation of the treasurer's book balance and the bank balance with a listing of outstanding checks and deposits in transit;
5. A balance sheet;
6. A statement of receipts and disbursements compared with the budget;
7. The auditor's certificate. This certificate may be as follows:

First Baptist Church
Any Place, Any State

> We have examined the balance sheet and the statement of receipts and disbursements for the general fund and the building reserve for the year ending December 31, _____. Our examination was made in accordance with instructions given in the chapter on the audit in *Church Finance System Record Manual* by Crowe and Moore and included such tests of the accounting records and such other auditing procedures as we consider necessary.
>
> In our opinion the attached balance sheet and statement of receipts and disbursements fairly set out the financial position of the church at December 31, _____, and the results of its operations for the year.

_____

_____

Auditors

There are other areas for control in the realm of administrative leadership, especially if one uses the concept of control as giving guidance. Several of the topics in the next chapter could just as well have been included as controls. This strategic functional area permeates almost all a church might attempt in its life and work.

The Church's Work Deserves to Be Done Decently and in Order

Serious Bible students know that Paul had some problems other than administration in mind when he wrote that in the church all things should be done decently and in order. Still, that truth could be well applied to administration. Paul painted a beautiful word picture of the church when he wrote in Ephesians 4 that

> We are to grow up in every way into him who is the head, into Christ, from whom the whole body, joined and knit together by every joint with which it is supplied, when each part is working properly, makes bodily growth and upbuilds itself in love (vv. 15-16, RSV).

Such a church as the Scriptures depict is a church worth working to produce. And such a church will make known the gospel, the manifold wisdom of God.

Summary

Administrative control is the last of the "functional areas" of church administration considered in this text. Strictly speaking, control is finding out what is happening—what is being accomplished—in relation to what was intended, and adjusting as needed to reach the desired results. More generally defined, control is the administrative guidance given to an enterprise, particularly through the use of tools or instruments for guidance.

Using the functional areas of administration as an organizing device, one can suggest numerous tools for giving administrative guidance to a church. Appreciation for controls usually is increased following some experience when things are out of control.

A church needs controls. It does not need the domineering control of any one person or of a group other than itself, under Christ. The church has the responsibility and the right to control that which is done in its name or by way of its resources. The intent of the illustrative instruments and suggestions in this chapter is to better enable the church to be the church, and to be more effective in that which it attempts.

Learning Activity Suggestions

1. Write your own definition of control as you would advocate applying controls in a church. How does your definition compare with those in this chapter?

2. Write your own job description in the position you now hold in church or the one for which you are preparing. Limit it to one page. Try to state it in terms of results for which you are responsible, rather than in terms of activities in which you might have responsibility.

3. What are the categories you would include in a comprehensive set of procedures for financial control in a church?

Notes

1. *Administrative Control and Executive Action*, eds., B. C. Lemke and James Don Edwards, (Columbus, Oh.: Charles E. Merrill Books, Inc., 1961), p. viii.

2. George R. Terry, *Principles of Management* (Homewood, Ill.: Richard D. Irwin, Inc., 1977, Seventh Edition), p. 481.

3. Edward C. Schleh, *Successful Executive Action* (Englewood Cliffs, N.J.: Prentice-Hall, Inc., 1955), pp. 52ff.

4. Charles Hickman Titus, *The Processes of Leadership* (Dubuque, Ia.: Wm. C. Brown Company, 1950).

5. J. M. Crowe and Merrill D. Moore, *Church Finance Record System Manual* (Nashville: Broadman Press, 1959), pp. 15-17.

6. Ibid., p. 17.

7. Ibid, pp. 31-32.

10
Basic Skills for Effective Administration

Leaders move their followers and followers are moved by their leaders. In contrast with the important function of leadership, the primary business of an organization often seems to be the conservation of those aspects of life which members have found good. The cluster is the conservator and therefore is conservative, bringing the full weight of its numbers to the support of the methods and instruments as they are. The organization insists upon the status quo. The leader urges movement.[1]

He also told them a parable: "Can a blind man lead a blind man? Will they not both fall into a pit?" (Luke 6:39, RSV).

Ideas This Chapter Includes

The importance of the leader

Basic skills of leadership

A leader's sources of strength

Importance of the Leader

Leaders make the difference, and training makes the difference in leaders. All leaders are born, but they are not born leaders. A leader must earn a following. One might be born to a leadership position or come to the position by appointment, election, military or other power, including a divine call. But what is given or attained in any access to a leadership position is no more than an opportunity for one to become the leader for which the position calls.

Leadership Requires Thought and Work

Some do indeed have more innate leadership potential than do others. Too, some come to the situtation requiring leadership at a time when leadership might be received and followed better than at other times. Still, leadership cannot be assumed to go with position per se, nor is it very likely to happen by accident. Most often when real leadership occurs, it comes as a result of intentional thought and work.

A Church Deserves and Requires Leaders and Leadership

A church needs leaders and leadership. It deserves and requires both. God has promised His church His presence and His leadership, along with His power and other resources. Among the resources He has given are people to lead. These people themselves are His gifts to churches; and the individual gifts they have been given come with the gift of themselves.

Leaders Must Earn a Following

It is true even of church leaders that their arrival at a position must be accompanied or followed soon by their earning a following. One might be in a leadership position in a church and not actually be a leader. *A leader is one who has followers.* There is no escaping that simple fact. No followers—no leader. And *leadership is what one does to get followers.* Certainly it is hoped that in a church, of all enterprises, the motivation of a leader will be more than just to have people following on a personal basis. In a church, as in other purposeful structures which are considerate of the dignity and worth of individuals, good leadership is more than mere leadership— getting people to follow. *Good leadership is working appropriately with other leaders and followers to determine outcomes that are desired and right and to progress cooperatively and effectively toward their realization.*

Basic Skills of Leadership

The kind of leaders and leaderships a church needs and deserves rarely appears by accident. Leaders must use certain skills to be good leaders. Skill is the ability to use one's knowledge effectively. It infers technical proficiency. It draws upon developed or acquired ability. Hence the truism that training makes the difference in leaders has meaning. There are leader skills in which one can develop or acquire some ability. It is imperative that church leaders offer no less than their best when the opportunity to lead comes to them. Church leaders must develop basic skills for leading.

There is no absolute list of criteria or qualities which can guarantee that their possessor will be a good leader. There are numerous books, even more articles, and other forms of media which are helpful in studying the making of a leader. But no one has yet discovered the guaranteed formula for success as a leader based on a list of traits. There are many ways to present the skills which a leader needs to employ to be effective.

In this chapter we will present and briefly comment about several skills which continue to contribute to the effectiveness of good leaders in churches, and whose absence continue to limit that effectiveness. These skills include planning, initiating, organizing, delegating, directing, motivating, supervising, performing, influencing, controlling, evaluating, communicating, and representing. A good and experienced leader, or a student of leaders and leadership, readily recognizes that this list is incomplete, overlapping, too ambitious for the space available for depth treatment, and doubtless reflects some other flaws. Nevertheless, there could be little doubt that the leader who does well at these skills would be well along the road to being a good and effective leader in a church.

Planning

Effective practitioners as well as scholars of leaders and leadership often rank *planning* as the most basic and essential skill for effective leadership. Planning usually begins with certain assumptions. It involves the gathering of information. It includes identifying and describing possible problems. It calls for consideration of options for solution. It demands making decisions today which will shape realities tomorrow.

Planning must be definite while remaining flexible to

changes which might later arise. Planning draws upon most of
the other skills leaders use. One must plan for planning itself,
and to communicate plans. One must plan for the planning to
be accepted. Then there remain the implementation dimensions. Truly, planning is a demanding, interdisciplinary skill
which no effective leader can long ignore and remain more
than the leader in name only, if indeed that can be retained.

Personal and group planning.—The general church leaders,
such as the pastor, other staff ministers, and leaders of church
programs need to learn to plan their personal leadership activities, as well as those activities which call for group planning.
There are at least two dimensions to almost every position of
leadership: those things which the leader does alone and those
which call for relating to others.

A prime illustration is the pastor and preaching. There
might be others who can also preach, but normally no one is
accepted as preacher quite to the extent as is the pastor. The
pastor must plan the preaching, usually without much involvement of others except the Holy Spirit. On another hand, there
are numerous instances in the life of a church in which the
pastor must plan with others. Whatever one might think of the
planning that goes into much preaching, many pastors seem to
have more difficulty with the planning that necessitates their
working with others. Perhaps a clue might be that in planning
to preach one has only oneself and, hopefully, the Lord to
consult; whereas in much of the other work of a church which
calls for planning, one must accommodate oneself to the reality of other persons. There are parallels in the pastor's administrative actions which the pastor alone can determine, and
there are those in which others must be taken into account.

In planning, as in many other skills, the pastor and other
church leaders must learn to work with people. Difficulties in
relating to others and working effectively together are not
limited to those who are church leaders. The difficulties in
working with others arise in every sector of group endeavor.
The hope should be that those in the service of the Lord and
the church might be good examples in this regard. Perhaps a
beginning point in meeting this area of need might be to
develop a wholesome understanding of and regard for self,

others, and the Lord. Such understanding and regard would put one in position to be not only a more effective planner but a more effective person in almost every area.

Initiating

Once plans are prepared, there is the need for skill in *initiating*. The best of plans is of little value unless it is installed and actuated. Someone or several persons must take the responsibility for initiating that which is planned. Some planning thoughts need to be given to determine the best ways to initiate plans once they are made.

Promotion

There is a fallacy which seems common to many church leaders about initiating. It is the fallacy of assuming that if the idea is good enough people will flock to support it or to otherwise relate appropriately to it whether or not someone takes the initiative. A word for this needed initiation might be promotion.

Promote means *to exalt in station, rank, or honor; to elevate; to advance.* It means to contribute to the growth or prosperity of; to further; as, to promote learning. For many, it seems, promotion in the church has come into disrepute. Perhaps one cause for this has been the frequent use of distasteful, huckstering approaches to promote. A church should have much which is worthy of promotion. Church leaders must find ways to advance the life and work of the church without going to the extremes of distasteful activities. Leaders must promote! They must initiate!

Chief leaders must promote.—One other emphasis might be helpful in relation to initiating and promoting. Just as the chief leaders of an enterprise, including a church, must involve themselves more than nominally in the planning process, so must they be more than nominally or passively involved in initiating and promoting. If a matter being promoted does not have more than passive interest to the chief leader, many will not come to regard the matter as something to which they wish to relate.

This is not to say that the pastor must be the most active

promoter of every church cause. But, almost without exception, any church cause in which the pastor's favor and support are not clearly perceived by the people is likely to have limited favor and support of the members. In some instances the favor and support of the pastor must come through not just on a single occasion but on a continuing basis. The pastor must not only help start things but also help keep them going. A church leader needs to develop the skill of initiating.

Organizing

The skill of *organizing* is a vital one for administrative leaders. Designing organizations can often be very complex. Those who lead in a church can hardly be effective without some organizing skills.

Organizing is deciding the pattern of relationships among persons who have a common task or purpose. In some instances in church life and work there might be limited help from history or precedent to guide in the organization design. But in many instances there are proven organization designs which would serve well. In such instances, leaders would be well advised to learn of these proven patterns and to consider whether or not these would meet the need most effectively. Decisions of this nature usually benefit from and, indeed, often require the participation of other persons in the church.

There is not an infinite number of ways to bring persons together organizationally. Sometimes a creative adjustment to some proven organizational pattern improves the structure. Occasionally there might be the need for a fresh start in the design of the organization. But most often, the creativity of leaders and members might be better focused on other areas of need, such as clarifying and communicating the purpose, the needs, the plan for ministry, and helping people to know how they might support and participate in the cause.

Avoid perpetual reorganizing.—Organization is a little like buildings and furnishings. One can spend an inordinate amount of time, energy, and other resources refurbishing buildings and rearranging the furniture and not affect the quality or the quantity of what happens very significantly. So it is with organization. Perhaps one reason some spend a lot of time reorganizing is that with organization, as with buildings and furnishings, it is easier to tinker than to address other more significant needs, because organization, buildings, and furnishings are less abstract and people encumbered than are some other areas. Continual, frequent changes of the design of organization can consume the interests and resources of people to the extent that they stay confused and less than productive. As with an automobile with a tire problem, the need is to find a wheel that rolls and use it and spend less time changing tires. Given a reasonable tolerance for adjustments, more people will move further along with less lost motion or inactivity.

Test new organization designs.—In addition to considering proven organization designs, leaders need to know about designing organizations. There are some suggestions in the chapter on organization in this book which apply. New designs need to be tested and proven worthy prior to their installation as the total organization. Such testing should continue for long enough to discover the strenghs and weaknesses as compared with the existing or upgraded present organization. Church leaders need to be continuing students of how to relate persons to one another effectively.

Delegating

Delegating is a skill which effective church administration leaders use well. It is the entrusting of a task to the care or management of another. Good delegating matches the assignment with the abilities of the person who receives the assignment. It also carries with it the freedom to act—the authority to carry out the assignment.

Once delegated, the delegator might check appropriately to see how the assignment is being carried out, but, except in very unusual circumstances, the assignment should be left with the one to whom it was given. Too many persons in administration take back delegated tasks at the first indication that the progress is less than the administrator expected or needed. In effective delegating there must be allowance for some variance from the rate or quality of productivity the leader might require from himself. There are also some possibilities that one to whom an assignment is made might even do it better than the leader who made the assignment!

Be aware of positions of persons in the organization.—Delegating calls for an awareness of the positions of persons in an organization. Typically, one delegates only to others who are under one's supervision in the organization. Peers in an organization often need to require certain assistance of one another. But a peer has the right of an assignment. Such is usually not the case as long as the assignment from a supervisor is moral and is related to the line of duty.

Accountability is another dimension of delegating. One who has received a delegated assignment is accountable to the supervisor for the performance of the task. A good delegator observes the rules of common courtesy in delegating, so that the assignment is not a personal demand but is a respectful request. Often in delegating it is helpful to get feedback to let the leader know that the assignment is clear. Too, it is often good to ask the person receiving the assignment to indicate the time by which the task will be completed.

Give away all you can and still be the leader.—A rule of thumb for effective administration in delegating is to give away any and all parts of the job which the leader can give away and clearly retain leadership. There are certain tasks which one cannot make a practice of delegating and remain the real leader. One part of being the leader which cannot be delegated is being the key influencer of critical decisions. Whoever forfeits being the key influencer of critical decisions forfeits leadership, if not the leadership position itself.

Another aspect which cannot be delegated is the role of chief ambassador or representative for the group one leads. Infrequently a leader might ask another to represent the group when normally the leader would do it. But if this becomes the routine practice, the leader forfeits the reality of leadership. Then, there might be a few tasks about a leader's job which the leader has the unique skills to perform to such an extent that it would be unfeasible or unwise to ask another to do them. The rest can be, and most often should be, delegated.

More a developer than a doer.—A common error which is a

hazard to delegating is continuing to do things which you perceive yourself to be good at doing or which you like to do for some other reason, but which could be done acceptably by someone in a subordinate position. Strangely, some who fall prey to this hazard actually think they are good at administration. What they are good at is performing some tasks included in administration. But a good administrator is not primarily a doer of things but a developer of people. An administrator develops people by helping them to succeed at doing their assignments. This itself is a major part of ministry. An effective administrator must learn to delegate well.

Directing

Directing is a skill which is essential for effective administration. It is of the order of instructing with authority. It is telling or otherwise indicating what others are to do. In ministry, whether among staff or volunteers, directing has its place, though not as often as some would like who enjoy directing others.

Directing is in order to implement tasks in which the one directing has the agreed-upon responsibility to direct and in which the situation requires someone to direct. This differs from a situation in which there is time and need for group participation in determining the direction. A music minister directs music groups by agreed-upon and understood authority in order to try to produce a certain effect. A minister of education directs certain educational projects in which plans have been made by group process and in which the minister of education has been determined to be the director. A pastor directs services of worship. A chairman directs a committee meeting with an agreed-upon agenda.

As with many other skills, winning or losing at being a good director depends heavily upon not only the knowledge of the director but also upon the director's personal relations with those directed and the manner in which direction is given. In church leadership one must always reflect Christian regard for those being directed. This is not to say that one should not direct forcefully and clearly. But verbally or otherwise assaulting persons under one's direction is unacceptable behavior for a Christian leader, even a designated director. A good director can indicate what others are to do in the group endeavor in a manner which gets the job done and which reflects proper esteem for all persons. This is not an easy skill to master, and there is always some risk of misunderstanding. Still, there are times when church administrative leaders must direct. It is a skill which requires cultivation on the part of the leader.

Motivating

An effective administrative leader needs to develop the skill of *motivating.* Contrary to a common misconception, motivation is not doing whatever is necessary to get others to do what we want them to do.

> A motive is what causes a person to act or to react. Motivation is the act of unleashing that within the individual which insights him to act or to react. When the unleashing is stimulated from within a person, we call it intrinsic motivation. When the stimulus is generated from without, as would be the case with the use of incentives, we call it extrinsic motivation. Intrinsic motivation, which many feel to be the purer kind, is like impulses or springs, often unrecognized or unconscious, providing impetus or driving power arising in oneself. Extrinsic motivation, considered by some to be less preferred in terms of ethics, is like an inducement, a spur, a goad, or an incentive, stimulating from outside oneself the internal impetus, causing one to act or to react.[2]

Suggestions for a Christian motivator. There are many studies and volumes of books on motivation. Perhaps an informal listing of some of the important considerations for a Christian motivator would help at this point.

1. Develop a wholesome and realistic self-concept.
2. Make or remake a personal policy decision: be honest, but not crude or indiscreet.
3. Generate and identify with worthy causes.
4. Behave consistently and predictably.
5. Communicate to the best of your ability.
6. Try to be an example of good.
7. Look at people positively, individually.

8.Put the need of the individual on a par, at least, with the task you might be influencing him or her to perform.
9.Assume that a person wants to do a good job, to complete his or her tasks.
10.Invite and accept peoples' genuine participation in group enterprises, even (or particularly) in the significant planning stages.
11.Work with the opposition.
12.Develop clear goals for yourself and for others.
13.Clarify expectations and standards with persons involved.
14.Show interest in and awareness of progress, whether in personal growth or in a task.
15.Run against your own clock, and allow others to do the same.[3]

The Christian administrator does not try simply to get people to do things. The best administrator tries to enable people to unleash their motivations to fulfill their own capabilities. As these responses can mesh with the needs of the group causes, they can contribute to effectiveness on the part of the leader. Work in this realm is risky, delicate, and personal. The effective Christian adminstrator recognizes this and works with these realities.

Supervising

An essential skill which is often shunned for a variety of reasons is *supervising.* This shunning is particularly evident in a church. There seems to be considerable reluctance in a church to give or to accept supervision, both among church staff persons and volunteer workers. This reluctance is a hindrance to both the personal development and to the productivity of all concerned.

Part of the problem that causes supervision to be so noticed by its absence or, in some instances, its abuse is doubtless an inadequate concept of supervision. Behind that is the general problem of leaders' concepts of self, others, and the Lord. Let us look at supervision itself.

Supervise comes from two Latin words, *super,* "over," and *videre,* "to see." The same term in biblical Greek is the word from which we get "bishop," *episkopos,* from *epi,* "over," plus *skopos,* "inspector." Our English words that include *vision* and *scope* come from these origins. In group enterprises or tasks there needs to be overseeing, inspecting. Some person or persons must perform this service to the individuals and their group. Therein lies one of the major difficulties: *in our culture we have not learned well how to distinguish the essential function of overseeing or inspecting from the status and authority of those who oversee or inspect.*

Many assume that the person who is supervising must obviously be a "super" *person,* or he or she would not be in that position. We must come to see supervision more as a service function than as a position reflecting superior personhood. Using levels to indicate supervisor-supervisee relationships contributes to the confusion. Each person must be viewed as the most important person in his or her own position, although the positions of supervisor and supervisee have obvious differences with respect to responsibility. One who can be secure enough as an individual to sort out personhood from function has a better opportunity to do well at supervising or at being supervised.

The best supervisors see their work as helping those supervised to develop as competent, growing persons and to perform their work well, as determined by reasonable and known standards and processes. In many situations, the standards and processes are best developed with meaningful participation by those who are to do the work. The supervisor is not a "snoopervisor." The supervisor works with those supervised to help both individuals and groups to be winners as persons and as producers. Often the person supervised is a better producer of his or her assignment than is the supervisor. Secure persons rejoice at this kind of situation. Supervising is a different task from being supervised. Each should rejoice when the other excels!

Supervising includes coordinating. It is a lot like a good quarterback on a football team who calls for adjustments at the line of scrimmage in order to run a successful play. There is an element of directing at this stage. There is control, there is communication, and many other skills. An effective administration leader needs to continue to develop skill at supervising. For further suggestions on this skill, see Appendix B.

Performing

The skill of *performing* is one which also requires command of other skills. As with a choir or an orchestra, there are times for solo performances and times for blending with the group. Confusion of these times distracts from the effectiveness of the overall effort.

Earlier in this chapter we mentioned that many jobs in leadership consist of some things which the individual must do alone and some things which call for working with and through other persons. In either aspect of your assignment, *you must get on with the doing of it. That is performing.* You can be capable of performing and not perform. You can have the needed knowledge to perform and not perform. You can attempt to perform without adequate preparation and usually do less than your best.

No one performs at maximum potential in every situation. It is general knowledge among those who minister that it is possible, even likely, that often you come to the end of a busy and productive day with a longer list of things calling for your attention than at the beginning of that day. New needs arise during any day, and old needs resurface.

Sometimes the best you can do is to give the best under the circumstances, all factors being considered. Our common humanity, the "milk of human kindness" regarding one another, and our love and trust toward one another help us through those times. When you are doing your best, assuming the match-up of the person and the task is right, you are performing. The best should be determined by your pattern and not by isolated or occasional instances of shortcomings. Such indicators as promptness, good effort, good attitude, and good follow through to completion are signals of good performance. Effective administrative leaders develop their skill of carrying on to the finish that which they are to do.

Influencing

The skill of *influencing* is an essential one for leaders. And it is one which is delicate and open to abuse. Some consider influence, like politics, predominantly with negative connotations. That is unfortunate. Here we mean for influencing to be the preferred concept rather than determining. *A leader should affect the significant decisions in the realm of one's responsibility, with limited use of official or individual power to determine by force or authority those decisions.*

Pastor.—The office of pastor has some power. The person in that office has some additional power. A church deserves, needs, and has the right to the influence of its pastor on significant matters in its life and work. A pastor needs to learn to use appropriately the power of the office and the personal power to influence the church to be and to do its best. The concept applies to others who lead.

A glaring abuse of influencing is seen in the persons who moderate or preside at a meeting and misuse the position to maneuver the body to accept or to do what it might not otherwise choose to accept or to do. Another abuse is the use of coercion beyond honest persuasion, either secretively or publicly. Neither these nor other such tactics have legitimate places in Christian leadership.

The best administrative leaders studiously avoid the abuse of their opportunities to influence. Rather they use them wisely in the best interests of all the body.

Informing.—Informing is one of the better ways to influence appropriately. A leader has the responsibility and must have opportunity to inform in situations where the information might make a difference. The intentional withholding of important information is a passive abuse of influencing which is out of place in a church. Leaders need to learn and to share information which will influence a church to make good decisions.

Controlling

Administrative leaders need the skill of *controlling*. This skill involves directing, guiding, restraining, keeping with limits. As we indicated in the chapter on administrative controls, we do not advocate the control of a single individual over the body, the church. What we do advocate is leaders helping the body to remain in control of itself. This is the skill which a leader needs to master.

Integrity, capability, truth, and right ideas.—One way to control in the sense we advocate is to maintain the confidence of the members in the integrity and the capability of the leader. Truth is much more in place as a force for control in a church than is the power of any office. The power of a right idea whose time has come is much to be preferred to any authoritarian edict by virtue of any office. There are some who make much of the authority of certain offices in a church. One who has to call attention to the authority of an office probably has not learned how rightly to use whatever powers the office authorizes. The most effective leaders learn to employ the power of truth as part of the skill of controlling. This means that the leader is always truthful.

Develop ways for the church to have control.—Another way to exercise the skill of controlling is to advocate and lead in developing, maintaining, and using appropriately the instruments of control of which we wrote in the chapter on administrative controls. In this sense the administrator is an executive. The leader is responsible for executing or supervising the will of the body of which he or she is the leader. A church needs to encourage the development, maintenance, and appropriate use of control instruments—policies, procedures, records, reports, and other devices—and to look to its leaders to execute the controls as instructed.

A service which an individual leader should render is to alert the body when things are approaching the danger of being out of control. In such a case, the leader might also come prepared with a suggested approach to modifying the course so that control is not lost. The leader can lead the body to take it from that point.

Evaluating

Evaluating is a skill which the effective administrator learns to use. Evaluating suggests an estimation of the worth, the usefulness, the value of something. There are certain principles of evaluating which democratic groups such as the church use.

Planners and implementers.—Persons involved in planning and carrying out plans should participate in any evaluation of the progress and accomplishment of plans. There is much to gain from the opinions of individuals not directly involved in the work being evaluated. In program evaluation, however, those who plan and implement activities are in the best position to relate the lessons of those experiences to the improvement of the future. These individuals know what they are seeking to accomplish. They can see more readily the significance of the weaknesses and strengths of the processes. They can better appraise the value of the results.

Develop evaluation criteria before implementing plans. —The full benefit of evaluation is not realized unless the tests to measure processes and products are set in advance. These tests—sometimes goals or standards—can have a beneficial effect on the performance itself. This is particularly true if the tests are worthy measurements. People like to measure up to expectations. It is more likely that they will measure up to a reasonable expectation if they know in advance what is expected. On the other hand, it is discouraging to learn that evaluation is being based on some measurement that was not known in advance of the appraisal.

Evaluate qualitatively and quantitatively.—Adequate evaluation takes into account more than one factor for measure of achievement. It is sometimes as essential to weigh as it is to count. Overall effectiveness can be more important than precise efficiency. A balance of concern with several factors, not always with equal emphasis, is vital to good evaluation.

Numbers are important, particularly if they represent people. Numbers that represent individuals are important because individuals are important.

Quality makes quantity meaningful. To neglect quantity or quality is to risk critical losses of both measures of achievement.

Time evaluation to get maximum benefit.—Premature evaluation can be damaging to success. It carries with it all the risks of predicting the future. Both extreme optimism and pessimism in evaluating too early can contribute to failure. Belated evaluation, too, is at times dangerous and at other times worthless. Leaders should determine the best time to evaluate in order to get the most benefit from their evaluation.

Evaluating during work performance allows time for modification of action. Progress checks illustrate this kind of evaluation. If progress can be stimulated by some coordinating adjustment, evaluation has served its purpose.

Evaluation when major phases or entire plans are finished is the postmortem analysis. Reviewing immediately after completing the actions allows a look at the tabulated results when memories are fresh. It is important to thorough evaluation that there not be too long a delay before the postmortem analysis.

Evaluate processes and results, not personalities.—Process evaluation has to do with the evaluation of means or methods —activities, organization, training, resources (such as equipment, materials, finances). Result evaluation concerns the outcome, the product of the process, the evaluation of ends realized. As church leaders evaluate, they should attack problems in these areas and avoid judging people. It is more important to discover through evaluation what the problems are than it is to place blame on persons.

Sometimes the problems are people. Even so, it is rarely, if ever, helpful to point out individual failures. A person under attack must find some way to protect himself. Defenses can be mounted and lines drawn between people that make future cooperative work difficult. Much of the value of evaluation is lost when personality conflicts enter the scene. Tactful avoidance of such conflicts leaves the way open to salvage erring workers who may learn to contribute significantly to future efforts.

Evaluate objectively and subjectively.—Objective and subjective evaluation have legitimate roles in evaluation. The objective approach uses the impersonal appraisal of statistical information. It is most useful in evaluating quantity. Numerical, statistical evidence best illustrates the objective approach.

The subjective approach depends primarily on personal evaluations by individuals. It is most useful in judging quality, especially since it relies on personal tastes, reactions, and opinions.

Communicate evaluation findings.—The greatest benefit in evaluation is not its historical significance but its present and future relevance. In the present it is a growth opportunity for those participating. In the future it offers insights that should make progress and success come more easily. Both the present benefits and those of the future depend on good communication of the evaluation.

People receive the benefit of evaluation only if they know what the findings are. It is more essential for some persons to receive this information than it is for others. Knowing who needs to know and getting the vital information to them is a leadership responsibility.

In conveying information, the positive should be accentuated, even in reporting a failure. There is value in dealing constructively with failure by pointing out weaknesses and suggesting possible ways either to avoid the weaknesses or overcome them in the future.

Insights should be written down for future reference. Memory is not adequate as a record of what is learned in evaluation. Sentiment sometimes replaces facts. Written copies of the findings that are pertinent can be valuable in planning for the future. Sometimes a secretary or recorder keeps more voluminous notes than are needful. Leaders can help determine what is essential for the record.

The important findings of evaluation can contribute to success of a present undertaking only if they are communicated in time. Progress reports and other similar checks can sometimes make the difference in victory or defeat. Leaders can be effective in stimulating progress through timely communciation of their findings.[4] It is important for the leader to learn this skill well.

Communicating

There is probably no skill which touches more areas of leadership more vitally than the skill of *communicating.* And there is probably no skill in which the total person and his or her behavior is more involved in the performance. Communication is truly the exchange of meanings from person to person. The body, the dress, the grooming, the expressions, the total appearance, the gestures, the symbols, the words—written or spoken or otherwise communicated—everything about a person has some part in the communicating realm. No administrative leader can reach his or her optimum and not be an effective communicator.

There are some troublesome paradoxes related to communication. For instance, with more available techniques, media, hardware, software, and other communication devices than in the entire previous history of the world, there seems to be less genuine understanding among persons than ever. A church should concern itself with genuine understanding of persons. It is essential that church leaders work at good communication.

Church office.—In addition to the individual responsibilities for communicating, about which the article in Appendix B speaks, there is need in the church for a communications center. Here we do not refer to a center for computers, the media library, or other very useful means. Here we have in mind the office services—the church office.

For most churches the church office is the point of contact most frequently used by those needing or seeking information. It actually has the potential of being the nerve center for communicating essential information among church members and other publics. Effective administrators consciously attempt to make this center the most informed and efficient point of contact in all the life of the church.

Communciating is indispensible in every functional area of administration: clarifying the purpose, determining the objectives, developing ministry plans, designing organization, administering human, physical, and financial resources, and in providing administrative controls. It is vitally related to all these skills and more: planning, initiating, organizing, delegating, directing, motivating, supervising, performing, influencing, controlling, evaluating, and representing. Administrative leaders who wish to be effective must continue to grow in their skill of communicating.

Representing

The last skill we shall treat here is *representing*. Again drawing upon many of those skills previously mentioned, the leader must give attention to the fact that he or she is usually considered to be the chief representative of the organization. Representing, or being the chief ambassador for one's organization is one of the skills and opportunities which cannot be delegated to another if the leader wishes to remain the real leader.

There is no escaping the fact that when people of the church or the community see the pastor, they most often think of the church. This is more often true regarding the pastor than of any other member. There are exceptions to this, but they are very rare indeed. Since this fact is at once an opportunity and a burden, the effective administrator tries to make it more often an opportunity.

The concept applies to other leaders as to their group identity. The leader who remains truly the leader must have some say about the points at which he or she will be the ambassador. Part of the effectiveness of a leader depends upon choosing judiciously the times to represent personally the cause and then doing it to the best of the leader's ability.

Leader's Sources of Strength

Where does a leader get the resources to cover all the areas of administration and to perform skillfully the responsibilities involved? This is a difficult question. The answer is even more difficult. At the risk of over-simplifying a very complex problem, let us suggest some sources of strength which each person must interpret and apply. Most of the details which comprise the answer might come from this group of suggestions.

Capability

One source of strength is *capability*. This has to do with native ability, reasonably good health, acceptable appearance, and basic intelligence, as well as some other assets. It should go almost without saying that one who has little capability of becoming an effective administrative leader is hardly likely to do so. But by no means do all who do have the basic ingredients try to become administrators; and not all who try become effective. Still, having the capability is an essential beginning.

Faithful Commitment

All the capability in the world, without *faithful commitment*, is vain and likely to fall short. This faithful commitment needs to be channeled in many directions, including the Lord, self, family, church, and others. It must include diligent work. It requires continuing, life-long learning. In ministering, this commitment involves calling and the leadership of God. Availability brings capability to this faithful commitment.

Integrity

Integrity is a source of strength the force of which cannot be overrated. A leader in a church cannot attain nor maintain effectiveness without a large measure of honesty of character, lack of duplicity, and authenticity. People turn most naturally for leadership to a leader who stands tall among others for the leader's own integrity.

Tensile Strength

Tensile strength is vital as a source for those who remain in ministry. In physics, tensile strength is the greatest longitudinal stress a substance can bear without tearing apart. Many a leader, even among church leaders and ministers, has exceeded the personal tensile strength and has been torn asunder. Many others have come very close to the breaking point.

A major illustration of this need for tensile strength is shown in Figure 1. It shows the necessity for church leaders themselves to be able to progress along the path of personal growth and leadership and still have the tensile strength to reach all the way back to the door of entry repeatedly to bring along the new followers. Many a leader has grown weary and too brittle to reach back repeatedly for the new followers, the slow-developing, longtime professors of the faith, and others for whom a leader must care. Some of those who have grown weary and too brittle have fallen to "burnout." No one is immune from this hazard.

One way to increase one's tensile strength is to reflect on the efforts and patience of the Lord and of others in bringing you along. All leaders need some reflecting times, for this and other needs.

The Lord

Another question seems fitting at this point. Where does one look for help in the gigantic matters which we have only partially addressed? The answer is easier to say than it is to appropriate. Nonetheless, the answer is essentially that one must depend upon the Holy Spirit with all one's might. It is as true today as at the time of its writing that our help comes from the Lord. It might come to us through others—family, friends, fellow church members, others—but the Source of sources is the Lord.

> I lift up my eyes to the hills.
> From whence does my help come?
> My help comes from the Lord, who made
>   heaven and earth.
>
> He will not let your foot be moved,
>   he who keeps you will not slumber.
> Behold, he who keeps Israel will
>   neither slumber nor sleep.
>
> The Lord is your keeper; the Lord
>   is your shade on your right hand.
> The sun shall not smite you by day,
>   nor the moon by night.
>
> The Lord will keep you from all evil;
>   he will keep your life.
> The Lord will keep your going out
>   and your coming in
>   from this time forth and for evermore
>   (Ps. 121, RSV).

Summary

Leaders are God's gifts to churches to enable churches to be what they can be and to do what they can do. Leaders bring with them certain gifts. These gifts are to be developed and used for the purpose of the church.

Figure 1

Tensile Strength of a Leader

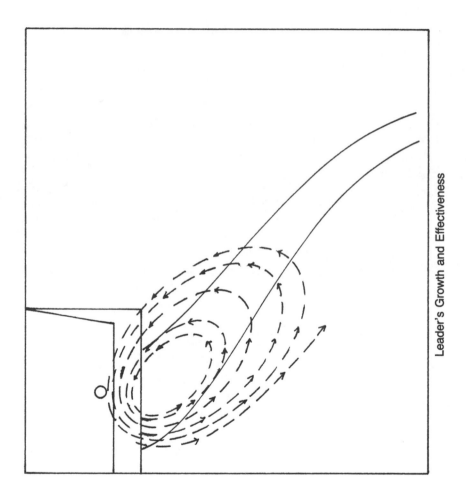

Leader's Growth and Effectiveness

At the lower left corner: The door of entry into fellowship—path of the leader and the distance of personal growth and effectiveness. The forward/upward line represents the leader's progress with self *and* followers. The return loop represents the necessity for the leader to have the tensile strength to keep returning to the door of entry to usher new followers along the path. The test: How far can a leader go on the path and retain the tensile strength to reach back to the door of entry for new followers?

Leaders have to earn their following. To do this well requires the exercise of leadership skills. Certain skills are known to contribute to the effectiveness of leaders in churches. These skills include planning, initiating, organizing, delegating, directing, motivating, supervising, performing, influencing, controlling, evaluating, communicating, and representing.

Effective leaders need resources for leadership. One framework upon which most of the needed resources can be attached includes capability, faithful commitment, integrity, and tensile strength. The most important resource is dependence upon the Holy Spirit. He is the Source of sources.

Learning Activity Suggestions

1. Write your own one-sentence definition of (1) leader and (2) leadership. How would you change your definitions to apply them to a church?

2. Write your own list of basic leadership skills. How would you arrange them in order of priority? How could a capable and faithfully committed person develop these skills?

3. Consider the section on tensile strength. From your experience or observation, what are three kinds of situations in church leadership which might test one's tensile strength? What are some possible approaches to increasing this tensile strength?

Notes

1. Charles Hickman Titus, *The Processes of Leadership* (Dubuque, Ia.: William C. Brown Company, 1950), pp. 349-350.

2. Lyle E. Schaller and Charles A. Tidwell, *Creative Church Administration* (Nashville: Abingdon, 1975), p. 67.

3. Ibid, pp. 77-80.

4. Charles A. Tidwell, *Working Together Through the Church Council* (Nashville: Convention Press, 1968), pp. 64-68.

Appendix A:
Sample Constitution and Bylaws

Constitution

Preamble

We declare and establish this constitution to preserve and secure the principles of our faith and to govern the body in an orderly manner. This constitution will preserve the liberties of each individual member and the freedom of action of this body in relation to other churches.

I. Name

This body shall be known as the _____ _____ Baptist Church of _____ _____, located at _____ _____ .

II. Objectives

To be a dynamic spiritual organism empowered by the Holy Spirit to share Christ with as many people as possible in our church, community, and throughout the world.

To be a worshiping fellowship, experiencing an awareness of God, recognizing His person, and responding in obedience to His leadership.

To experience an increasingly meaningful fellowship with God and fellow believers.

To help people experience a growing knowledge of God and mankind.

To be a church which ministers unselfishly to persons in the community and the world in Jesus' name.

To be a church whose purpose is to be Christlike in our daily living by emphasizing total commitment of life, personality, and possessions to the lordship of Christ.

III. Statement of Basic Beliefs

We affirm the Holy Bible as the inspired Word of God and the basis for our beliefs. This church subscribes to the doctrinal statement of "The Baptist Faith and Message" as adopted by the Southern Baptist Convention in 1963. We voluntarily band ourselves together as a body of baptized believers in Jesus Christ personally committed to sharing the good news of salvation to lost mankind. The ordinances of the church are believer's baptism and the Lord's Supper. (See article VI of the Bylaws.)

IV. Church Covenant

Having been led as we believe by the Spirit of God to receive the Lord Jesus Christ as our Lord and Savior and, on the profession of our faith, having been baptized in the name of the Father, and of the Son, and of the Holy Spirit, we do now in the presence of God and this assembly most solemnly and joyfully enter into covenant with one another as one body in Christ.

We engage, therefore, by the aid of the Holy Spirit to walk together in Christian love; to strive for the advancement of this church in knowledge, holiness, and comfort; to promote its prosperity and spirituality; to sustain its worship, ordinances, doctrines, and discipline; to contribute cheerfully and regularly to the support of the ministry, the expenses of the church, the relief of the poor, and the spread of the gospel through all nations.

We also engage to maintain family and secret devotions; to religiously educate our children; to seek the salvation of our kindred and acquaintances; to walk circumspectly in the world; to be just in our dealings, faithful in our engagements, and exemplary in our deportment; to avoid all tattling, backbiting, and excessive anger; to abstain from the sale of and use of intoxicating drinks as a beverage; to use our influence to combat the abuse of drugs and the spread of pornography; and to be zealous in our efforts to advance the kingdom of our Savior.

We further engage to watch over one another in brotherly love; to remember one another in prayer; to aid one another in sickness and distress; to cultivate Christian sympathy in feeling and Christian courtesy in speech; to be slow to take offense, but always ready for reconciliation and mindful of the rules of our Savior to secure it without delay.

We moreover engage that when we remove from this place, we will as soon as possible unite with some other church where we can carry out the spirit of this covenant and the principles of God's Word.

V. Polity and Relationships

The government of this church is vested in the body of believers who compose it. Persons duly received by the members shall constitute the membership. (See article I of the Bylaws.)

All internal groups created and empowered by the church shall report to and be accountable only to the church, unless otherwise specified by church action.

This church is subject to the control of no other ecclesiastical body, but it recognizes and sustains the obligations of mutual counsel and cooperation which are common among Baptist churches. Insofar as is practical, this church will cooperate with and support the association, the state convention, and the Southern Baptist Convention.

Bylaws

I. Church Membership

Section. 1. General

This is a sovereign and democratic Baptist church under the lordship of Jesus Christ. The membership retains unto itself the exclusive right of self-government in all phases of the spiritual and temporal life of this church.

The membership reserves the exclusive right to determine who shall be members of this church and the conditions of such membership.

Section 2. Candidacy

Any person may offer himself as a candidate for membership in this church. All such candidates shall be presented to the church at any regular church service for membership in any of the following ways:

(1) By profession of faith and for baptism according to the policies of this church.

(2) By promise of a letter of recommendation from another Baptist church.

(3) By restoration upon a statement of prior conversion experience and baptism in a Baptist church when no letter is obtainable.

Should there be any dissent as to any candidate, such dissent shall be referred to the membership committee for investigation and the making of a recommendation to the church within thirty (30) days. A three-fourths vote of those church members present and voting shall be required to elect such candidates to membership.

Section 3. New Member Orientation

New members of this church are expected to participate in the church's new member orientation.

Section 4. Rights of Members

(1) Every member of the church is entitled to vote at all elections and on all questions submitted to the church in conference, provided the member is present or provision has been made for absentee balloting.

(2) Every member of the church is eligible for consideration by the membership as candidates for elective offices in the church.

(3) Every member of the church may participate in the ordinances of the church as administered by the church.

Membership shall be terminated in the following ways: (1) death of the member, (2) dismission to another Baptist church,

(3) exclusion by action of this church, or (4) erasure upon request, or proof of membership in a church of another denomination.

Section 5. Discipline

It shall be the practice of this church to emphasize to its members that every reasonable measure will be taken to assist any troubled member. The pastor, other members of the church staff, and deacons are available for counsel and guidance. The attitude of members toward one another shall be guided by concern for redemption rather than punishment.

Should some serious condition exist which would cause a member to become a liability to the general welfare of the church, the pastor and the deacons will take every reasonable measure to resolve the problem in accord with Matthew 18. If it becomes necessary for the church to take action to exclude a member, a two-thirds vote of the members present is required; and the church may proceed to declare the person to be no longer in the membership of the church. All such proceedings shall be pervaded by a spirit of Christian kindness and forbearance.

The church may restore to membership any person previously excluded, upon request of the excluded person, and by vote of the church upon evidence of the excluded person's repentance and reformation.

II. Church Officers and Committees

All who serve as officers of the church and those who serve on church committees shall be members of this church.

Section 1. Church Officers

The officers of this church shall be the pastor, the church staff, the deacons, a moderator, a clerk, a treasurer, and trustees.

(1) The pastor is responsible for leading the church to function as a New Testament church. The pastor will lead the congregation, the organizations, and the church staff to perform the appropriate tasks.

The pastor is leader of pastoral ministries in the church. As such he works with the deacons and church staff to: (1) lead the church in the achievement of its mission, (2) proclaim the gospel to believers and unbelievers, and (3) care for the church's members and other persons in the community.

A pastor shall be chosen and called by the church whenever a vacancy occurs. The election shall take place at a meeting called for that purpose, of which at least one week's public notice has been given.

A pastor selection committee shall be elected by the church to seek out a suitable pastor, and its recommendations shall constitute a nomination. Any church member has the privilege of making other nominations according to the policy established by the church. The committee shall bring to the consideration of the church only one name at a time. Election shall be by ballot, an affirmative vote of three fourths of those present being necessary for a choice. The pastor, thus elected, shall serve until the relationship is terminated by his request or the church's request. He shall preside at meetings of this church, and if so designated may serve as moderator in all business meetings in keeping with the rules of order authorized in these bylaws.

The pastor may relinquish the office as pastor by giving at least two weeks' notice to the church at the time of resignation. The church may then declare the office of pastor to be vacant. Such actions shall take place at a meeting called for that purpose, of which at least one week's public notice has been given. The meeting may be called upon the recommendation of a majority of the personnel committee and the deacons, or by written petition signed by not less than one fourth of the resident church members. The moderator for this meeting shall be designated by the members present by majority vote, and he shall be someone other than the pastor. The vote to declare the office vacant shall be by ballot; an affirmative vote of two-thirds of the members present being necessary to declare the office vacant. Except in instances of gross misconduct by the pastor so excluded from office, the church will compensate the pastor with not less than one twelfth of his total annual compensation. The termination shall be immediate and the compensation shall be rendered in not more than thirty days.

(2) The ministerial staff shall be called and employed as the church determines the need for such offices. A job description shall be written when the need for a staff member is determined. Those staff members of whom the church requires evidence of a personal call of God to minister shall be recommended to the church by the personnel committee and called by church action. At the time of resignation at least two weeks' notice shall be given to the church. The church may vote to vacate such positions upon recommendation of the personnel committee, such termination being immediate and the compensation conditions being the same as for the pastor, except that the amount shall relate to the individual's compensation.

Nonministerial staff members shall be employed as the church determines the need for their services. The church personnel committee shall have the authority to employ and to terminate services of nonministerial staff members. Such employment and termination of services shall be with the recommendation of the supervising staff member and, as appropriate, with the consultation of related committees of the church.

(3) The church shall elect deacons by ballot at regular business meetings of the church. There shall be one deacon elected for assigned service for every twelve to fifteen church families.

Deacons shall serve on a rotating basis. Each year the assigned term of office of one third of the number of deacons shall expire, and election shall be held to fill vacancies and to add to the deacons such numbers as the church size warrants. In case of death or removal or incapacity to serve, the church may elect a deacon to fill the unexpired term. After serving a term of three years' assignment, a deacon shall be eligible for reelection only after the lapse of at least one year. There shall be no obligation to constitute as an assigned deacon one who has been a deacon in another church; but in such instances as one might be chosen by this church for assignment as a deacon, his previous ordination by another church of like faith and order shall suffice for this church.

In accordance with the meaning of the work and the practice in the New Testament, deacons are to be servants of the church. Their task is to serve with the pastor and staff in performing the pastoral ministries tasks of (1) leading the church in the achievement of its mission, (2) proclaiming the gospel to believers and unbelievers, and (3) caring for the church's members and other persons in the community.

(4) The church shall elect annually a moderator as its presiding officer. In the absence of the moderator, the chairman of deacons shall preside; or in the absence of both, the clerk shall call the church to order and preside for the election of an acting moderator.

(5) The church shall elect annually a clerk as its clerical officer. The clerk shall be responsible for keeping a suitable record of all official actions of the church, except as otherwise herein provided. The clerk shall be responsible for keeping a register of names of members, with dates of admission, dismission, death, or erasure, together with a record of baptisms. The clerk shall issue letters of dismission voted by the church, preserve on file all communications and written official reports, and give required notice of all meetings where notice is necessary, as indicated in these bylaws. The clerk shall be responsible for preparing the annual letter of the church to the association.

The church may delegate some of the clerical responsibilities to a church secretary who will assist the elected clerk. All church records are church property and shall be kept in the church office when an office is maintained.

(6) The church shall elect annually a church treasurer as its financial officer. It shall be the duty of the treasurer to receive, preserve, and pay out—upon receipt of vouchers approved and signed by authorized personnel—all money or things of value paid or given to the church, keeping at all times an itemized account of all receipts and disbursements. It shall be the duty of the treasurer to render to the church at each regular business meeting an itemized report of the receipts and disbursements of the preceding month. The treasurer's report and records shall be audited annually by an auditing committee or public accountant. The treasurer shall be bonded at the church's expense.

Upon rendering the annual account at the end of each fiscal year and its acceptance and approval by the church, the records shall be delivered by the treasurer to the church clerk, who shall keep and preserve the account as part of the permanent records of the church.

(7) The church shall elect three or more trustees to serve as legal officers for the church. They shall hold in trust the church property. Upon a specific vote of the church authorizing each action, they shall have the power to buy, sell, mortgage, lease, or transfer any church property. When the signatures of trustees are required, they shall sign legal documents involving the sale, mortgage, purchase, or rental of property, or other legal documents related to church-approved matters.

Trustees shall serve on a rotating basis, with one new trustee being elected every three years.

Section 2. Church Committees

The committees of this church shall be a nominating committee, a personnel committee, a church property and space committee, a stewardship committee, a missions committee, and such other regular and special committees as may be added by the amendment procedures prescribed within these bylaws. All church committee members shall be recommended by the church nominating committee and elected by the church unless otherwise specified within these bylaws. Committee members shall serve on a three-year rotating basis with one third to be elected each year.

(1) The nominating committee coordinates the staffing of all church leadership positions filled by volunteer workers, unless otherwise specified herein. Persons considered for any such positions shall first be approved by the nominating committee before they are approached for recruitment. The nominating committee shall present to the church for election all who accept the invitation to serve.

(2) The personnel committee assists the church in matters related to employed personnel administration, including those called by church action. Their work includes such areas as determining staff needs, employment, salaries, benefits, other compensation, policies, job descriptions, and personnel services.

(3) The church property and space committee assists the

church in matters related to properties administration. Its work includes such areas as maintaining all church properties for ready use, recommending policies regarding use of properties, consulting with the personnel committee and the church staff about the needs for and the employment of maintenance personnel, and the assignment of supervisory responsibility to appropriate personnel.

(4) The stewardship committee develops and recommends an overall stewardship development plan, a unified church budget, and budget subscription plans. It advises and recommends in the administration of the gifts of church members and others, using sound principles of financial management. It works with the treasurer in the preparation and presentation to the church of required reports regarding the financial affairs of the church.

(5) The missions committee seeks to discover possibilities for local missions projects, shares findings with church program organizations, and serves the church in establishing and conducting such missions projects as may be assigned to it.

III. Basic Church Programs

The church shall maintain programs of Bible teaching; church member training; church leader training; new member orientation; mission education, action, and support; and music education, training, and performance. All organizations related to the church programs shall be under church control, all officers being elected by the church and reporting regularly to the church, and all program activities subject to church coordination and approval. The church shall provide the human resources, the physical resources, and the financial resources for the appropriate advancement of these programs.

(1) The Sunday School shall be the basic organization for the Bible teaching program. Its tasks shall be to reach persons for Bible study; teach the Bible; witness to persons about Christ and lead persons into church membership; minister to Sunday School members and nonmembers; lead members to worship; interpret and undergird the work of the church and the denomination.

The Sunday School shall be organized by departments and/

or classes, as appropriate for all ages, and shall be conducted under the direction of the Sunday School director elected by the church.

(2) The Church Training organization shall serve as the training unit of the church. Its tasks shall be to equip church members for discipleship and personal ministry; to teach Christian theology and Baptist doctrine, Christian ethics, Christian history, and church polity and organization; to equip leaders for service; and to interpret and undergird the work of the church and the denomination.

Church Training shall be organized by departments for all ages and conducted under the direction of a general director.

(3) Woman's Missionary Union shall be the mission education, mission action, and mission support organization of the church for women, young women, girls, and preschool children. Its tasks shall be to teach missions; engage in mission action and personal witnessing; support missions; and interpret and undergird the work of the church and the denomination.

Woman's Missionary Union shall have such officers and organizations as the program requires.

(4) The Brotherhood shall be the church's organization for mission education, mission action, and mission support for men, young men, and boys. Its tasks shall be to engage in mission activities; teach missions; pray for and give to missions; develop personal ministry; and interpret and undergird the work of the church and the denomination.

The Brotherhood shall have such officers and organization as the program requires.

(5) The church music organization, under the direction of the church-elected music director, shall be the music education, training, and performance organization of the church. Its tasks shall be to provide musical experiences in congregational services; develop musical skills, attitudes, and understandings; to witness and minister through music; and to interpret and undergird the work of the church and the denomination.

The church music program shall have such officers and organization as the program requires.

IV. Service Programs

The church shall maintain media library services and recreation services for the purpose of enriching and extending the ministries and programs of the church and administrative services as in article II.

(1) The media library service will be the resource center for the church. Its personnel will seek to provide and promote the use of printed and audiovisual resources. They also will provide consultation to church leaders and members in the use of printed and audiovisual resources.

(2) The church recreation service will seek to meet the recreational needs of members and groups. Its personnel will provide recreation activities, consultation, leadership assistance, and resource.

V. Church Council

The Church Council shall serve the church by leading in planning, coordinating, conducting, and evaluating the ministries and programs of the church and its organizations.

The primary functions of the Church Council shall be to recommend to the church suggested objectives and church goals; to review and coordinate ministry and program plans recommended by church officers, organizations and committees; to recommend to the church the use of leadership, calendar time, and other resources according to program priorities; and to evaluate achievements in terms of church objectives and goals.

Regular members of the Church Council shall be the pastor, other church staff members, directors of church program organizations, media library director, recreation director, chairman of deacons, church officers, and chairmen of church committees.

All matters agreed upon by the council which call for action not already approved shall be referred to the church for approval or disapproval.

VI. Church Ordinances

Section 1. Baptism

This church shall receive for baptism any person who has received Jesus Christ as Savior by personal faith, who professes Him publicly at any worship service, and who indicates a commitment to follow Christ as Lord.

(1) Baptism shall be by immersion in water.

(2) The pastor, or whomever the church shall authorize, shall administer baptism. The deacons shall assist in the preparation for, and the observance of baptism.

(3) Baptism shall be administered as an act of worship during any worship service of the church.

(4) A person who professes Christ and is not baptized after a reasonable length of time shall be counseled by the pastor and/or staff or deacons. If negative interest is ascertained on the part of the candidate, he shall be deleted from those awaiting baptism.

Section 2. The Lord's Supper

The church shall observe the Lord's Supper quarterly, the first Sunday of the quarter, unless otherwise scheduled by the church. The observance shall alternate between the morning and the evening services of worship. The pastor and deacons shall administer the Lord's Supper, the deacons being responsible for the physical preparations.

VII. Church Meetings

Section 1. Worship Services

The church shall meet regularly each Sunday morning, Sunday evening, and Wednesday evening for the worship of Almighty God. Prayer, praise, preaching, instruction, and evangelism shall be among the ingredients of these services. The pastor shall direct the services for all the church members and for all others who may choose to attend.

Section 2. Special Services

Revival services and any other church meetings essential to the advancement of the church's objectives shall be placed on the church calendar.

Section 3. Regular Business Meetings

The church shall hold regular business meetings monthly on a designated Wednesday night.

Section 4. Special Business Meetings

The church may conduct called business meetings to consider matters of special nature and significance. A one-week notice must be given for the specially called business meeting unless extreme urgency renders such notice impractical. The notice shall include the subject, date, time, and place; and it must be given in such a manner that all resident members have opportunity to know of the meeting.

Section 5. Quorum

The quorum consists of the members who attend the business meeting, provided it is a stated meeting or one that has been properly called.

Section 6. Parliamentary Rules

Robert's Rules of Order, Revised is the authority for parliamentary rules of procedure for all business meetings of the church.

VIII. Church Finances

Section 1. Budget

The stewardship committee, in consultation with the Church Council, shall prepare and submit to the church for approval an inclusive budget, indicating by items the amount needed and sought for all local and other expenses. Offering envelopes will be provided for members' use.

It is understood that membership in this church involves financial obligation to support the church and its causes with regular, proportionate gifts. Annually there shall be opportunity provided to secure worthy commitments of financial support from the church members.

Section 2. Accounting Procedures

All funds received for any and all purposes shall pass through the hands of the church treasurer, or financial secretary, and be properly recorded on the books of the church. Those who have responsibility that involves actual handling of funds shall be bonded, the church paying for the bond. (See article II, section 1, (6), regarding the church treasurer.)

A system of accounting that will adequately provide for the handling of all funds shall be the responsibility of the stewardship committee.

Section 3. Fiscal Year

The church fiscal year shall run concurrently with the calendar year.

IX. Church Operations Manual

A special committee of the church shall develop a church operations manual to include church policies and procedures and organization charts depicting lines of responsibility in the administration of the church. The manual shall be kept in the church office and made available for use there by any member of the church. A church secretary shall maintain the manual. The Church Council or a special committee shall review the manual at least annually, with authority to recommend changes for the church to consider. Any church member or church organization may initiate suggested changes in the manual.

Addition, revision, or deletion of church policies requires: (1) the recommendation of the church officer or organization to whose areas of assignment the policy relates, (2) discussion by the Church Council, and (3) approval by the church.

Procedures may be added, revised, or deleted by: (1) recommendation of the church officer or organization to whose areas of assignment the procedures relate, (2) approval by the Church Council, and (3) approval of the church, if the Church Council deems it necessary.

X. Amendments

Changes in the constitution and bylaws may be made at any regular business meeting of the church provided each amendment shall have been presented in writing at a previous business meeting and copies of the proposed amendment shall have been furnished to each member present at the earlier meeting. Amendments to the constitution shall be by two-thirds vote of church members present. Amendments to the bylaws shall have a concurrence of a majority of the members present and voting.

Appendix B:
Decalogue for Supervisors

Moses' "ten words" are indelibly inscribed on the fabric of history. This decalogue could possibly help supervisors to be delivered "out of the house of slavery" (Ex. 20:2, NASB).

I. *Thou shalt establish and maintain adequate communication.* The chief of a staff is primarily responsible for making this "commandment" a reality. Every staff member has a share of this responsibility, but the major initiative is the responsibility of the supervisor.

The implications of this command range from the giving of clear instructions by the supervisor to the feedback and suggestion flow from those supervised. There must be free and easily usable communications in all relational directions, or the communication is inadequate. The supervisor is the single most significant figure in making adequate communication a reality.

For example, one technique which helps assure that a worker understands a supervisor's request is the "echo" technique. Follow up given instruction, a work directive or request, by asking the worker to repeat the instructions. This technique might be useful in reverse, too, when receiving information from a worker.

Make it easy, even inviting, for workers to give feedback—their honest impressions, even about the supervisor's ideas. And don't miss getting the workers' suggestions, even the unusable ones. A worker whose unusable ideas are received will likely feel free to offer other ideas. Some of these might be good.

Avoid the C-R-U-D syndrome—"Communication Restricted Unilaterally Downward." There must be ample freedom for workers to relate to persons anywhere in the organization for purposes of communication without suspicion or fear. The supervisor must have a very secure personality for adequate communication to be achieved.

II. *Thou shalt set clear and reasonable deadlines.* If deadlines are involved at all, they should be known by the worker at or near the beginning of an assignment. One way to help assure clear and reasonable deadlines is to ask the worker to suggest the time by which he thinks the assignment can be completed. If this time can be accepted by the supervisor, everyone is ahead.

Workers grow weary and sometimes resentful of unreal deadlines and of work assignments regularly imposed on too short notice. On the other hand, they usually feel more responsible for meeting deadlines they themselves help set.

III. *Thou shalt check appropriately on progress.* Ask workers how they are coming on work assignments. Avoid embarrassing workers. Be sure you don't nag by asking too soon or too frequently. Take care about asking in the presence of others. Supervision can degenerate easily to "snoopervision." Give the leeway needed for workers to work effectively without feeling harrassed.

Different workers need your interest at different intervals. Even the same worker might need your, "How are you doing on . . .?" more frequently on some assignments than on others. To learn to do this effectively, the supervisor must get to know his people and know generally what is involved in their work.

Sometimes you might need to keep a log of work assignments made, along with the progress at certain critical points, the time of expected completion, and the actual completion time. Such a log could help not only with operational supervision but also with worker development interviews and salary appraisals.

IV. *Thou shalt make needed help available.* Often when a supervisor asks, "How are you coming on . . .?" a worker reflects the need for help. Perhaps they need more time, more workers, more information or training, more material, different working conditions, different equipment, more money, less interference, more freedom, or any of a number of things.

The supervisor must assess the need, probably with the worker involved and possibly many others. If the need is valid and a solution can be advanced, the supervisor must see that the help is made available.

V. *Thou shalt encourage workers to seek help, responsibly.* Encourage workers to feel free to seek help when they have the need. Discourage their coming to you or seeking help on every little matter. The supervisor's door must be open, at least unlocked, so workers have access when they need help. When a worker has a problem, the supervisor has a problem, whether he knows it yet or not. Most often it is better to know and to support the worker in the situation.

VI. *Thou shalt develop solution-minded workers.* A supervisor's beatitude might be: "Blessed is the worker who suggests one or more possible solutions to every problem he brings." Usually there is a workable solution to the problems encountered in a work situation. Help the worker feel responsible for finding possible options, not just locating or identifying obstacles. When a worker brings a problem to you, ask what he would suggest as a possible answer. Unless you have a significantly better answer, accept the one suggested.

If a worker does not seem to have an answer, and if time permits, suggest he think further about it and come up with one or two suggestions. Set a time in your own thinking by which you will check with him to see if he has solved the problem. Or ask him to let you know when he has a possible solution. Commend him for good effort in finding answers. Acknowledge obstacles identified, but avoid commendation for mere identification of obstacles. Encourage the pursuit of solutions. He will soon get the idea.

You don't have to labor under the burden of feeling you must have answers to every problem. Your workers can become creative solvers of problems and can multiply productivity.

VII. *Thou shalt attack problems, not people.* You solve problems by attacking problems. In supervising you don't solve problems by attacking people. Attacking people almost always complicates the problem situation. It does not develop people, and it reduces productivity.

People need to be encouraged, not put down. Don't say, "Bert, I've told you numerous times that you need to, . . ." or "Bert, how many times must I tell you that . . .?" Rather, say, "Bert, I notice that there is still a problem regarding . . . What do you suppose might be tried next?" or "What do you suppose might be an answer to this problem?" Direct the worker's energies toward solving the problem.

Avoid putting the worker on the defensive so that he consumes his best thinking energy protecting himself. For a normal person, survival is fundamental and becomes a primary concern when under personal attack. The worker under attack is at least partially a diminished person—you've cut away some part of him. And the problem is not solved either. Lay off!

VIII. *Thou shalt time guidance for optimum good.* Give guidance at the earliest appropriate time. If the task is such that you can risk letting the cycle of the situation run its full course, you might defer guidance until after the assignment is completed and offer it in a routine evaluation session. Sometimes, though, you must supervise early in a sequence of events in order to salvage a situation you can't afford to overlook.

Rarely should you deal with a worker on a sensitive problem while others are present. Wait, if you can, and handle it privately with the person involved. You might set a "wait limit," setting a time limit to allow the worker to recognize and to acknowledge the problem and to take the initiative to come for guidance. After the "wait limit" you must take the initiative. But remember the seventh "commandment."

IX. *Thou shalt avoid trivia.* Supervise. Give guidance on those matters which affect the success of the worker or of the work. This sometimes makes the work more interesting.

Discover those margins of error you can tolerate and still develop the workers and produce the work. Actively enter the situation when the margins of error are in joepardy, or are actually exceeded. Overlook minor variations that don't cost too dearly. Evaluate the results, the end products, not every little indicator en route. Don't be "picky."

X. *Thou shalt learn from mistakes.* The lessons of experience should be instructive. Often the "tuition" we pay for these lessons is expensive. Why not get the message, and try to avoid making the same mistakes repeatedly?

Identify problems that occur again and again as you evaluate the work. Anticipate how you will avoid repeating mistakes. Develop policies and procedures to help you know in advance what you will do in repeated similar circumstances.

Try to lead your workers to suggest the policies and procedures they feel suit the situation. After all, if you are really a supervisor, your workers do the actual producing, not you. Your job is to produce the kind of setting and to give the kind of guidance that will *enable* them to become the persons they are capable of becoming, under God, and to do the work they are capable of doing. (—Adapted from article by Charles A. Tidwell, *Church Administration,* April 1977, pp. 3, 7; volume 18, number 7.)

Keep Communications Open

How can people working together establish and continue to keep open their lines of communication? What are some ways the church staff can become more effective in communicating with one another and with others?

The following suggestions are designed to provide some answers to these questions.

Decide to be a communicating person. Try to grow in being open. Share, don't hoard information. Provide means of communication and encourage their use. Use the tools you have for communication. Write memos. Share copies of correspondence as needed. Conduct regular staff meetings and conferences.

Take the risks involved in trusting others. After all, most of those with whom you work have the same kind of commitment, the same Father, Lord, Savior. Be trustworthy and discover that more people will come to trust you.

Affirm a policy of openness of information and practice it. Give up the special personal pleasure of thinking you know something others don't know and delighting in their efforts at guessing what it is. Be a communicating person.

Study communication. Learn what is and what is not communication.

Communication is behavior that results in an exchange of meaning, according to David K. Berlo in *The Process of Communication.*

Communication is behavior. That covers every action from a wrinkled brow or a faraway look of detachment to a physical gesture or a spoken statement. It might be written, pictured, written-pictures (like a cartoon), symbolic pictorial (like a cross or a dove), symbolic audio (like a chime or a recording of instrumental music or a bell), audiovisual (like a motion picture with sound), or it might be face-to-face audio communication behavior. Many times this is the best medium. It might be intermediate audio (like a conversation on the telephone or on an intercom system).

Communication is not just telling. It is not just announcing or writing a notice in a bulletin. There is really no communication unless there is some kind of response. As one comic said, communication without response is like a yo-yo without the second yo. Comm:unciation that is restricted to one direction is not communication.

Learn the process of communication. At this point the one attempting to initiate an exchange of meaning chooses some vehicle or vehicles for conveying the meaning: a word, an act, a symbol, a gesture, or some other means. He puts the meaning into some "code"—he encodes.

Next the initiator *sends* the message. He transmits the meaning via the vehicle previously chosen.

Then comes the receiving of the message—either as initially encoded and sent with some distortion.

The receiving person then *decodes* the impact. He "translates" what he thinks he receives into what he thinks the initiator sent. Many factors affect this decoding phase: light, darkness, time of day, weather, health, experience, history, age, personality, and other affectors.

Finally the receiver, after decoding, *responds.* If all has gone well in the process, good communication occurs: a bona fide exchange of meaning. Then, on occasion, the cycle repeats itself.

One who learns and works diligently at improving his skills

in the process of communication has a better chance of really communicating than does one who is not aware of the process.

Distinguish what you support from what you know. The following story and "test" can help you see how easy it is to confuse supposition and knowledge. Check yourself on this story by reading the story carefully one time and then circling the answer you believe to be accurate. After completing the exercise, go back to the account and see how you relate what you supposed with what you knew.

A church member was counting the receipts from the morning offering when he was called to the telephone by a church worker. When he returned he found nothing on the table at which he was working. He quickly called the town's police captain.

1. The telephone rang after the deacon began counting receipts?   T   F?
2. The man counting the receipts was a church member.   T   F?
3. After talking on the phone, the church member returned to the counting table.   T   F?
4. The church member was working at the table.   T   F?
5. The money he was counting had disappeared when he returned from the telephone conversation.   T   F?
6. Someone called the deacon to the phone.   T   F?
7. The church member was not counting the morning's receipts.   T   F?
8. The church member telephoned the town's police captain to report a robbery.   T   F?
9. The story involves the deacon, the church member, and the police captain.   T   F?
10. This is what happened: money was being counted, the telephone rang, the deacon went to answer the phone, someone stole the money, and the police were called to investigate.   T   F?

(Check your answers against the story. How many did you *suppose* and how many did you *know?*)

Try to choose direct words. Avoid ambiguous words—words with high potential for conveying other meanings than what is intended.

Words really don't have meaning. People do. Someone who counts things like this has reported that the five hundred most frequently used words in the English language have more than fourteen thousand dictionary definitions.

It takes careful, often deliberate, effort to choose words which accurately convey meaning from one person to another.

Develop your learnability. Avoid building a "know-it-all wall." Look, listen, learn. Don't feel compelled to have a ready answer for every question. As "know-it-all-ness" increases, learnability decreases and vice versa. The result is personal nongrowth, rather than growth. Besides, you block communication with others as your "know-it-all wall" grows between you.

See people as individuals. Avoid lumping them together. Each person is unique. Those who preassign persons to caricatured categories cannot communicate well with individuals. Those who say, "All pastors act that way," or "All ministers of education have this characteristic," or "All ministers of music tend to have that problem," or "All secretaries, all custodians, . . ." and on it could go.

Don't be a victim of "hardening of the categories."

Solve a potential problem as it arises. Don't let problems accumulate until you get emotionally wrought up about them.

One technique that helps "keep the air clear" among staffers working together is to ask good faith questions about the potential problem. Questions like these will often defuse a possible foul-up in communication:

Is this really what appears to be happening?
If so, is that what we think should be happening?
What might be done to correct the situation?
Who needs to be the one(s) to do what needs to be done?
If the one who needs to act is not in the group asking the question, then who will get the word to him?

Pick your problems to attack. Ignore the problems that don't matter much anyway. Focus on those that are significant. Use your powers sparingly and with appropriate timing.

The best of communications networks, hardware, skills cannot make up for the absence of Christian love and trust. Pray together. Suffer together. Work together. Rejoice together. Love and trust grow in these elements. So will your communication. (Adapted from an article by Charles A. Tidwell, *Church Administration*, January 1978, pp. 8-10; Volume 20, Number 4.)

Bibliography

Books

Allen, Louis A. *The Management Profession.* New York: McGraw-Hill, 1964.

Anderton, T. Lee. *Church Property/Building Guidebook.* Nashville: Convention Press, 1980.

Appley, Lawrence A. *The Management Evolution.* United States of America: American Management Association, Inc., 1963.

Bratten, J. D. *Tough-Minded Management.* New York: American Management Association, 1963.

Beal, Will, comp. *The Work of the Minister of Education.* Nashville: Convention Press, 1976.

Bennett, Jr., Frank Russell. *The Fellowship of Kindred Minds: A Socio-Theological Study of Baptist Association.* Atlanta, Ga.: Home Mission Board, Southern Baptist Convention, n.d.

Bingham, Robert E. *Traps to Avoid in Good Administration.* Nashville: Broadman Press, 1979.

Brown, Jerry W. *Church Staff Teams That Win.* Nashville: Convention Press, 1979.

Carver, W. O. *The Glory of God in the Christian Calling.* Nashville: Broadman Press, 1949.

Colson, Howard P. and Raymond M. Rigdon. *Understanding*

Your Church's Curriculum. Rev. ed. Nashville: Broadman Press, 1981.

Crowe, J. M. and Merrill D. Moore. *Church Finance Record System Manual.* Nashville: Broadman Press, 1959.

Dale, Bob. *Growing a Loving Church.* Nashville: Convention Press, 1974.

Dean, Robert James, chairman, editorial committee. *Encyclopedia of Southern Baptists,* Vol. IV. Nashville: Broadman Press, 1982.

Dobbins, Gaines S. *Learning to Lead.* Nashville: Broadman Press, 1968.

Engstrom, Ted W. *The Making of a Christian Leader.* Grand Rapids: Zondervan Publishing House, 1976.

Foshee, Howard B. *The Ministry of the Deacon.* Nashville: Convention Press, 1968.

Foshee, Howard B., et al. *The Work of Church Officers and Committees.* Nashville: Convention Press, 1968.

Graves, Allen W. *Principles of Administration for a Baptist Association.* Atlanta, Ga.: Home Mission Board, Southern Baptist Convention, n.d.

Gray, Robert N. *Managing the Church,* vol. I and II. Enid, Okla.: The Phillips University Press, 1971.

Grubbs, Bruce. *Helping a Small Church Grow.* Nashville: Convention Press, 1980.

Harmon, Nolan B. *Ministerial Ethics and Etiquette.* Nashville: Abingdon Press, 1950.

Haugen, Edmund. *Mister/Madam Chairman.* Minneapolis: Augsburg Publishing House, 1963.

Hendricks, William L. *Resources Unlimited.* Nashville: Stewardship Commission of the Southern Baptist Convention, 1972.

Hendrix, Olan. *Management for the Christian.* Milford, Mich.: Mott Media, 1981.

Hiltner, Seward. *Ferment in the Ministry.* Nashville: Abingdon Press, 1969.

Hobbs, Herschel H. *The Baptist Faith and Message.* Nashville: Convention Press, 1971.

Howington, Nolan. "Church Back Design Revision." unpublished paper July 20, 1978.

Hughes, Charles. *Goal Setting: Key to Individual and Organizational Effectiveness.* New York: American Management Association, 1965.

Lemke, B. C. and James Don Edwards, ed. *Administrative Control and Executive Action.* Columbus, Oh.: Charles E. Merrill Books, Inc., 1961.

Lindgren, Alvin J. *Foundations for Purposeful Church Administration.* New York: Abingdon Press, 1965.

Lindgren, Alvin J. and Norman Shawchuck. *Management for Your Church.* Nashville: Abingdon Press, 1977.

McDonough, Reginald M., comp. *A Church on Mission.* Nashville: Convention Press, 1980.

McDonough, Reginald M. *Growing Ministers, Growing Churches.* Nashville: Convention Press, 1980.

McDonough, Reginald M. *Keys to Effective Motivation.* Nashville: Broadman Press, 1979.

McDonough, Reginald M. *Working with Volunteer Leaders in the Church.* Nashville: Broadman Press, 1976.

Mosley, Ernest E., comp. *Leadership Profiles from Bible Personalities.* Nashville: Broadman Press, 1979.

Mosley, Ernest E. *Priorities in Ministry.* Nashville: Convention Press, 1978.

Myers, Marvin, *Managing the Business Affairs of a Church.* Nashville: Convention Press, 1981.

Powers, Bruce P., ed. /comp. *Christian Education Handbook.* Nashville: Broadman Press, 1981.

Preston, Mary Francis Johnson. *Christian Leadership.* Nashville: Convention Press, 1955.

Ray, Cecil. *How to Specialize in Christian Living.* Nashville: Convention Press, 1982.

Ray, Cecil. *Living the Responsible Life.* Nashville: Convention Press, 1974.

Robertson, A. T. *A Harmony of the Gospels for Students of the Life of Christ.* New York: Harper and Brothers, 1950.

Schaller, Lyle E. and Charles A. Tidwell. *Creative Church Administration.* Nashville: Abingdon Press, 1975.

Schlek, Edward C. *Successful Executive Action.* Englewood Cliffs, N.J.: Prentice Hall, Inc., 1955.

Sheffield, James A. *Church Officer and Committee Guidebook.* Nashville: Convention Press, 1976.

Short, Jr., Mark. *The Bible and Business.* Nashville: Broadman Press, 1978.

Smith, Elliott. *Advance of Baptist Associations Across America.* Nashville: Broadman Press, 1979.

Sullivan, James L. *Baptist Polity.* Nashville: Broadman Press, 1983.

Terry, George R. *Principles of Management* (7th ed.) Homewood, Ill., Richard D. Irwin, Inc., 1970.

Tidwell, Charles A. *The Educational Ministry of a Church.* Nashville: Broadman Press, 1982.

Tidwell, Charles A. *Training Potential Sunday School Workers.* Nashville: Convention Press, 1976.

Tidwell, Charles A. *Working Together Through the Church Council.* Nashville: Convention Press, 1968.

Titus, Charles Hickman. *The Processes of Leadership.* Dubuque, Ia.: William C. Brown Co., 1950.

Torbet, Robert G. *A History of the Baptists.* Philadelphia: The Judson Press, 1950.

Vieth, Paul H. *Objectives in Religious Education.* New York: Harper and Brothers, 1930.

Watson, Emerson Cleveland. *Associational Base Design.* Atlanta, Ga.: Home Mission Board of the Southern Baptist Convention, n.d.

Wedel, Leonard E. *Church Staff Administration.* Nashville: Broadman Press, 1978.

Young, Robert A. *The Development of a Church Manual of Administrative Policies.* Louisville: Bel-Air Studios Church Directory Pub., n.d.

Periodicals

Clark, George, ed. *Church Administration.* Nashville: Sunday School Board of the Southern Baptist Convention, published monthly.

Hayes, Judi Slayden, ed. *Search.* Nashville: Sunday School Board of the Southern Baptist Convention, published quarterly.

Holck, Jr., Manfred, ed. *Church Management: The Clergy Journal.* P. O. Box 1625, Austin, Tex., 78767.

Merrill, Dean, ed. "Leadership." *Christianity Today,* Inc., 465 Gundersen Drive, Carol Stream, Ill., 60187.

Pamphlets

Nine Steps in Starting New Churches. Atlanta, Ga.: Home Mission Board of the Soutern Baptist Convention, 1983.

Tidwell, Charles A. *The Church Constitution and Bylaws Committee.* Nashville: The Sunday School Board of the Southern Baptist Convention, 1977.